A GRIMOIRE OF T[
Volume 2. Psalm[

Dr. Lazarus Corbeaux
2019

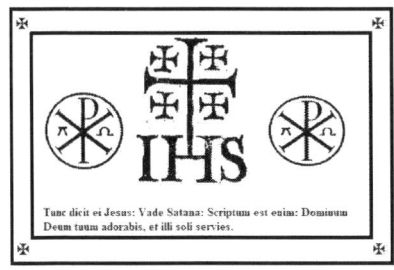

COPYRIGHT & DISCLAIMER

A Grimoire of the Psalms Volume 2. Psalms 51-100

© 2019 Laci Metheny

No part of this book may be reproduced in any written, electronic, recording, or photocopying without the written permission of the author.

This book is not intended as a substitute for medical, legal, or any other professional advice. The reader should regularly consult a physician in regards to the matter of his/her health and particularly in regards to any symptoms that may require diagnosis and medical attention. The reader should also consult licensed legal professionals in regards to any matters of the law, whether criminal or civil. Neither the author nor the publishers assume any liability for the use, or misuse, of any of the information provided in this text. It is presented as an academic study of folklore, and neither the author nor the publisher will assume any liability for damages of any kind, that may result from the use of the information presented here.

CONTACT

Facebook:
http://www.facebook.com/drcorbeauxsconjureroom

Wordpress:
http://www.drcorbeaux.wordpress.com

Youtube:
http://www.youtube.com/user/thetoadsbool

Email: drcorbeaux@gmail.com

+BMN+ATD+OFYL+
Amen
+++
I
N
R
I
INRI + INRI
I

```
      N
      R
      I
```

INRI✠OW✠C✠T✠B✠SB✠W✠IHVH

A NOTE ON THE TEXT

The order of the Psalms will be based upon the King James Version of the Bible, as it is the most widespread, so to use this text you will need either a KJV Bible or one of the small New Testaments that contain the Book of Psalms.

The Psalm number will be presented in the left hand corner, followed by the specific seals, talismans, and workings that relate to that Psalm.

May God bless you in your work,
Dr. Lazarus Corbeaux

+++

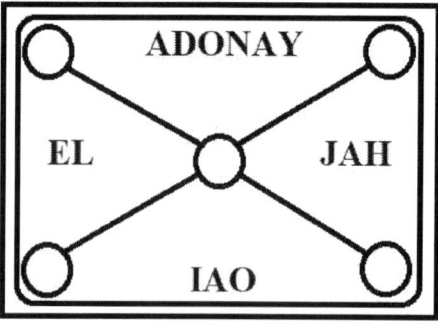

PSALM 51

UNCROSSING

Make the above square on cloth and pray the psalm over it to make a prayer cloth. Carry this near your heart to remove crossed conditions.

TO CHANGE BAD LUCK TO GOOD

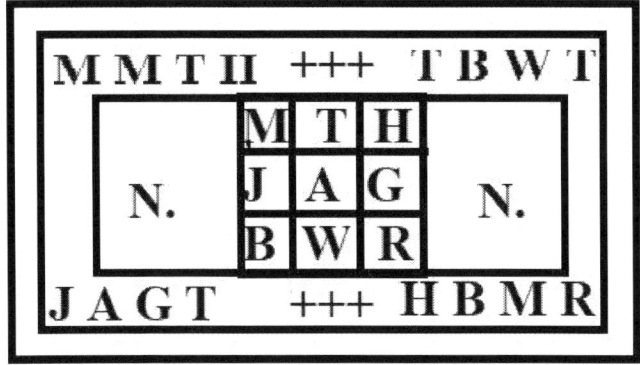

Make the above seal on clean parchment and hold it in your left hand during a Mass. After the mass, when the final benediction is given, place the seal in your right hand. Collect some holy water on your way out, go home and burn the seal to ashes. Mix the seal in with the holy water, and drink it in three sips in the name of the Father, Son, and Holy Ghost.

TO BRING CONVERSION TO A SINNER

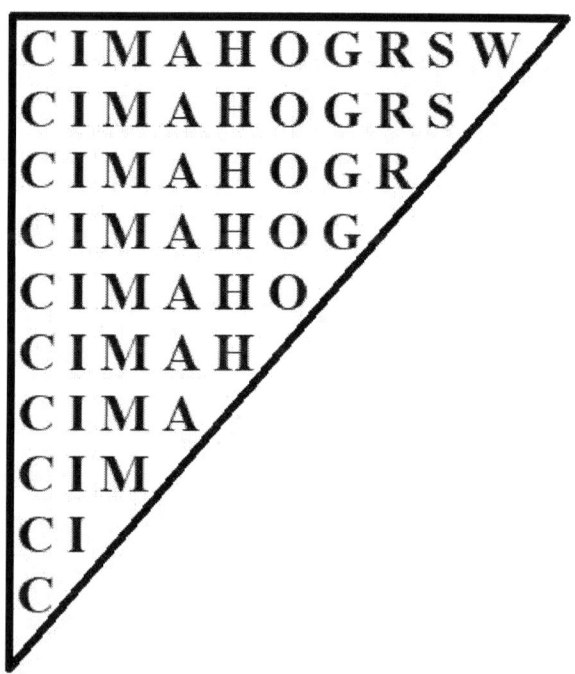

Draw the above triangle over a photograph of the person. Recite the psalm over the photo every night for nine nights, between which you will keep the photograph inside a bible.

TO MEND A BROKEN RELATIONSHIP

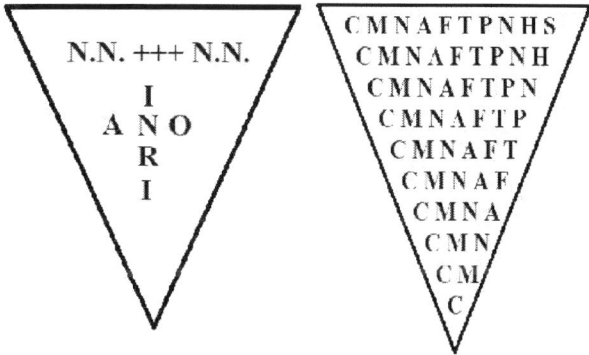

Mark the above seal on copper, during the Day and Hour of Venus, replacing N.N. and N.N. with your name and the name of your partner. Over this seal, the psalm is prayed 7 times, and it is anointed with rose oil and carried wrapped in green silk.

FOR LARYNGITIS AND SORE THROAT

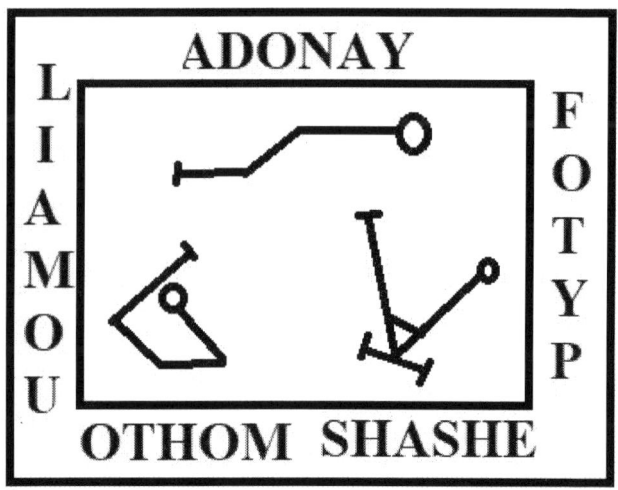

Make the above seal on parchment, pray the psalm three times over it, and wear it around the throat.

PROTECTION

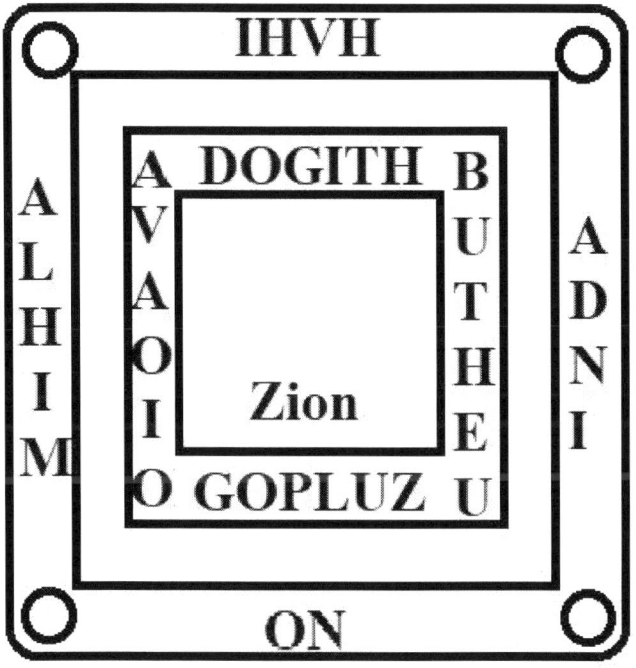

Make the above seal on a new plate. At the four corners, within the circle, light a white candle. Say the psalm four times, and carry the plate clockwise around the area you wish to protect. Then place the plate in the center, and allow the candles to burn down. Afterwards, hide the plate in a high place, such as the attic crawl space.

PSALM 52

FOR THE ARROGANT

Fashion the above seal on lead, replacing N.N. with the name of the arrogant individual to be brought down. Pray the psalm nine times over it and bury it, facing down, in the grave of a male child that did not live past nine days.

TO BRING JUSTICE UPON A LIAR

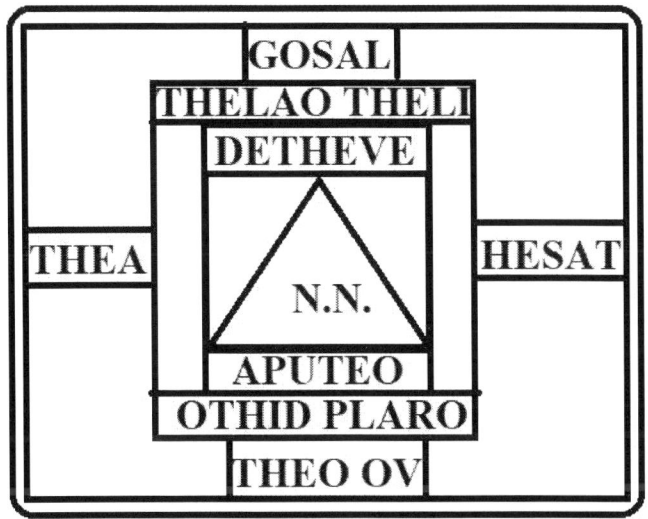

Make the above seal on clean parchment, replacing N.N. with the name of the person. Recite the psalm nine times over the seal, during the day and hour of Saturn. Place the seal inside an earthen jar, with a piece of pork. Bury the jar at the west side of the cemetery.

FOR ASSISTANCE AGAINST RICH AND INFLUENTIAL ENEMIES

Mark the above seal and consecrate it with the psalm three times in the name of the Most Holy Trinity. Carry it near your heart.

PSALM 53

TO MAKE YOUR ENEMIES FEAR YOU

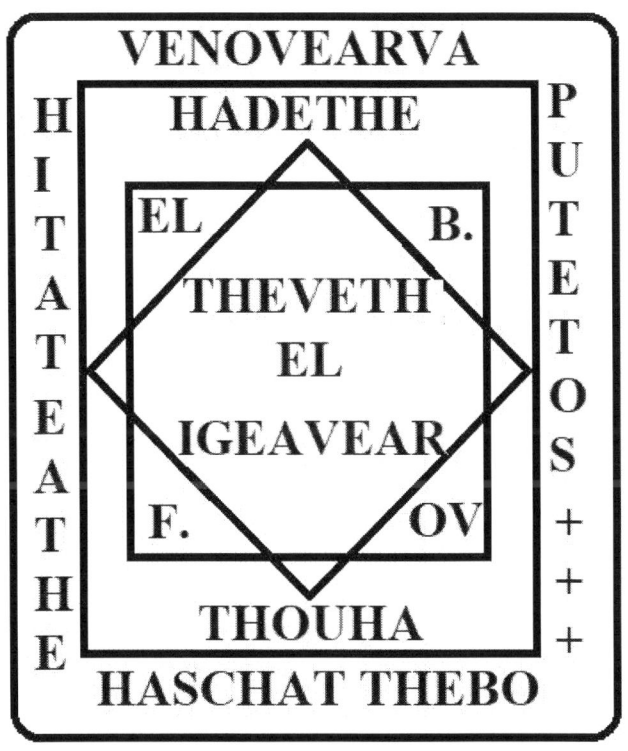

Carry the above seal, fashioned in silver on the day and hour of the Moon with the psalm prayed over it three times in honor of the Most Holy Trinity.

FOR THE RELEASE OF A PRISONER

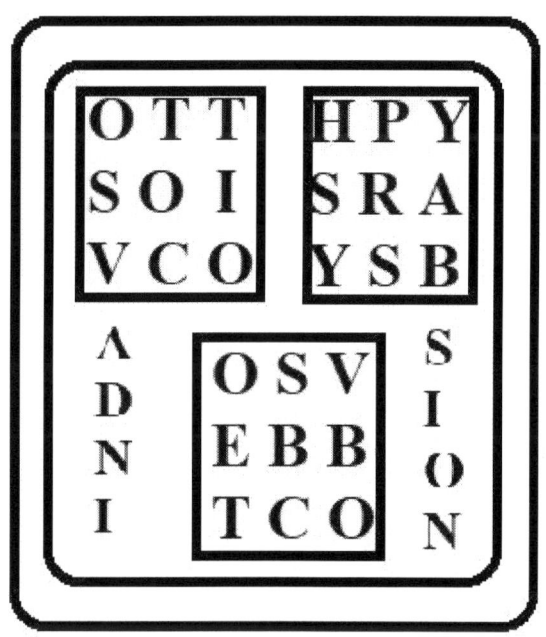

Fashion the above seal on aluminum and on the back write the name of the prisoner, with their mother's name, and their birthdate.

Every day, take the seal and pray the psalm three times over it while facing east. When not being prayed over, hang the seal on the eastern wall of their room, or any room in the home. But it is preferred it if is the room they will dwell in upon their release.

PSALM 54

FOR JUSTICE AGAINST ENEMIES

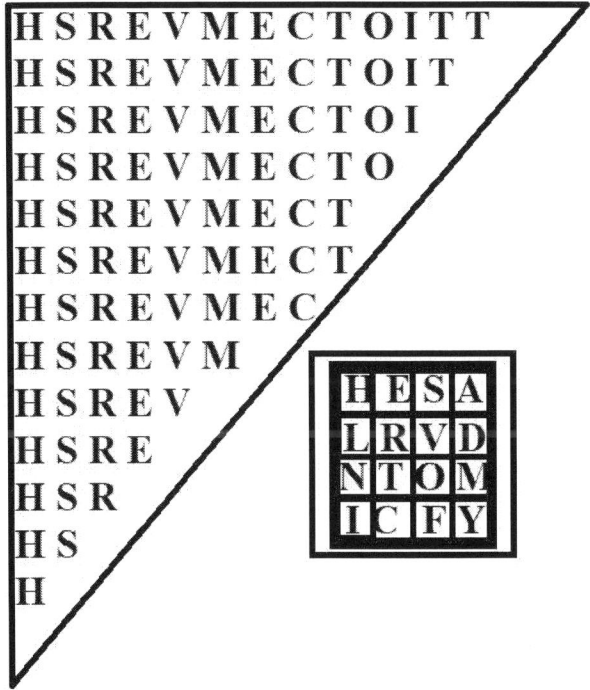

Make the above triangle on clean paper, and the square upon the back. Pray the psalm nine times over the seal. Burn the seal to ashes and throw it over your left shoulder into running water.

TO INFLUENCE ANOTHER

Mark the above seal on copper or brass. When you wish to influence a person, with ink write their initials within the circle and pray the psalm seven times over it. When you wish to release them, wash away the initials with holy water.

TO REMOVE TROUBLES

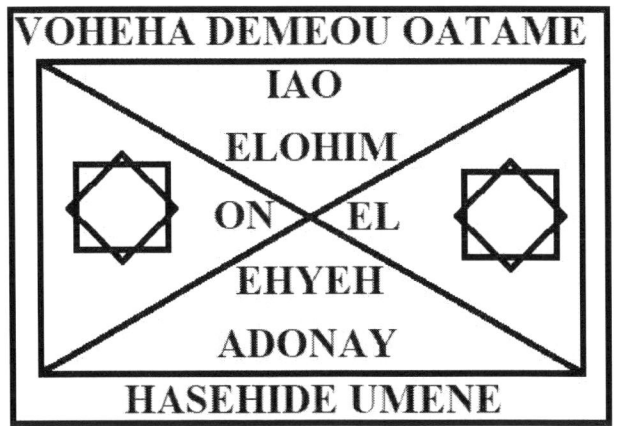

Make the following seal on clean parchment and every day for seven days at dawn, pray the psalm over it facing east. After the seventh recitation, burn the seal to ashes, mix with rain water, and drink it.

PSALM 55

TO MAKE PEOPLE SEEK YOU OUT AND OBEY YOUR WORDS

Mark the above seal and consecrate it with the psalm 7 times. Wear the seal around your throat.

TO STRIKE TERROR, FEAR, AND PARANOIA IN AN ENEMY

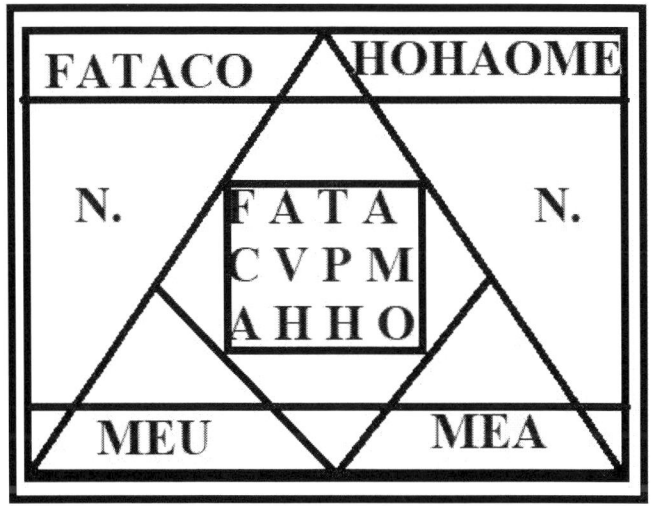

The above seal is written in ink fashioned from iron oxide and water from a thunderstorm. The N. and N. are replaced with the name of the enemy. The psalm is prayed over it 5 times, for the head, both arms, and both legs of your enemy. The seal is afterwards burned to ashes, and the ashes deposited where they shall come in contact with your enemy.

TO MAKE A PERSON LEAVE

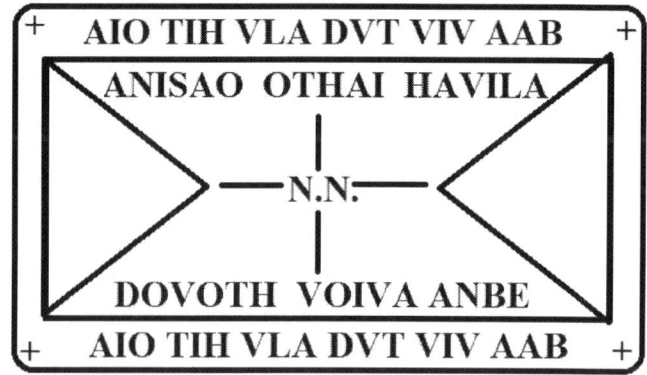

Write the above psalm on paper, replacing N.N. with the name of the person you wish to leave. The psalm is prayed over the seal three times, after each recitation saying the person's name and the words on the seal: **ANISAO OTHAI HAVILA DOVOTH VOIVA ANBE.** After which, the seal is left at a crossroads away from you and your normal routes of travel.

TO BANISH A STORM

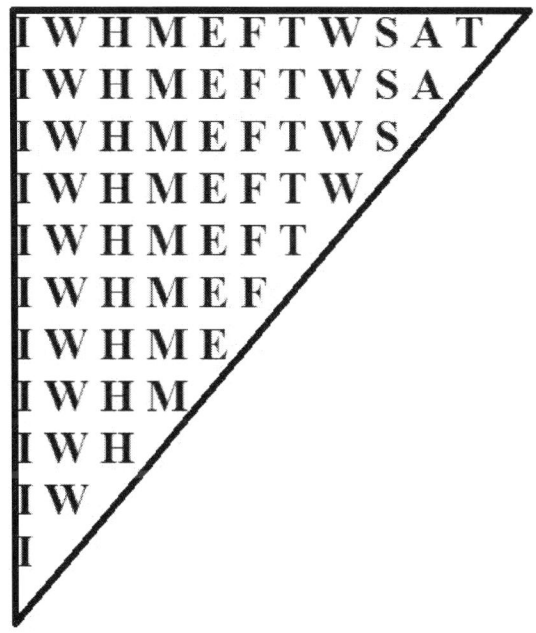

Write the above triangle on nine slips of paper. Pray the psalm, and burn one paper. Repeat for each nine triangles.

TO DESTROY CONSPIRACIES AGAINST YOU

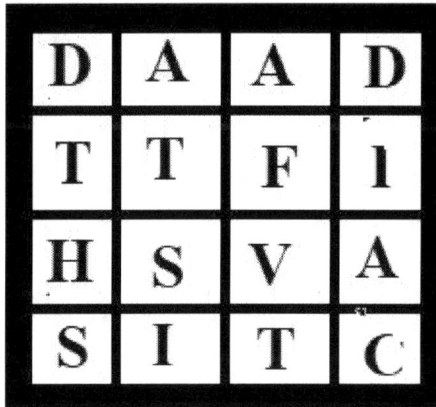

Carry the above seal, consecrated with the psalm five times, on your person. Those who conspire against you, will begin conspiring against each other, and fall apart.

TO DESTROY AN ENEMY

```
L D S V T A G Q I H F W
L D S V T A G Q I H F
L D S V T A G Q I H
L D S V T A G Q I
L D S V T A G Q
L D S V T A G
L D S V T A
L D S V T
L D S V
L D S
L D
L
```

Write the above triangle on seven pieces of parchment. Whisper the enemy's name over each piece.

```
┌─────────────────────────┐
│  LEDESEV THALETH        │
│  GODOQI HEVOVI          │
│  ITHEDA ATHE            │
└─────────────────────────┘
```

The above seal is made on an earthen jar in black ink.

On the night of the New Moon, take the seven triangles and pray the psalm seven times, dropping one triangle in at a time. Afterwards, fill the jar with soured wine and leave it at the gates of the cemetery.

FOR PROTECTION IN BATTLE

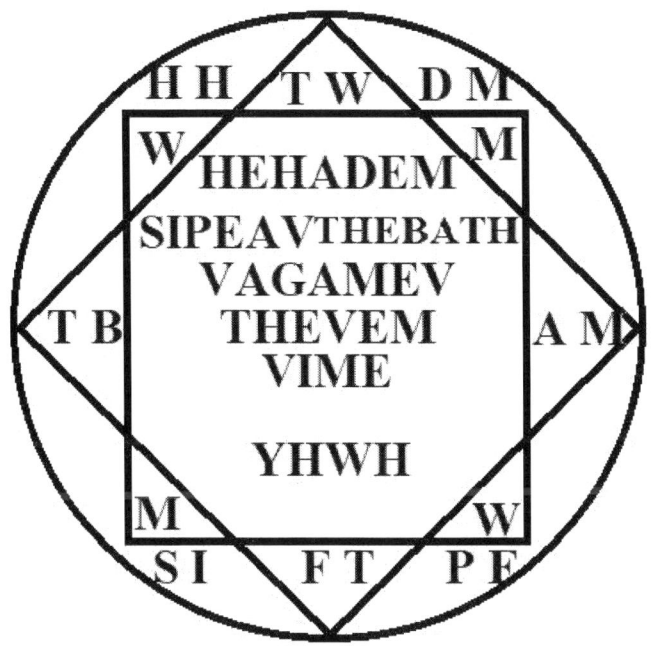

Carry this seal when going into battle. Cross yourself with it and recite the psalm, then carry it next to your heart.

PSALM 56

FOR RECOVERY FROM ILLNESS

Make the psalm on clean parchment and consecrate it with the psalm nine times. Have the patient wear it on their person.

TO TURN BACK ENEMIES

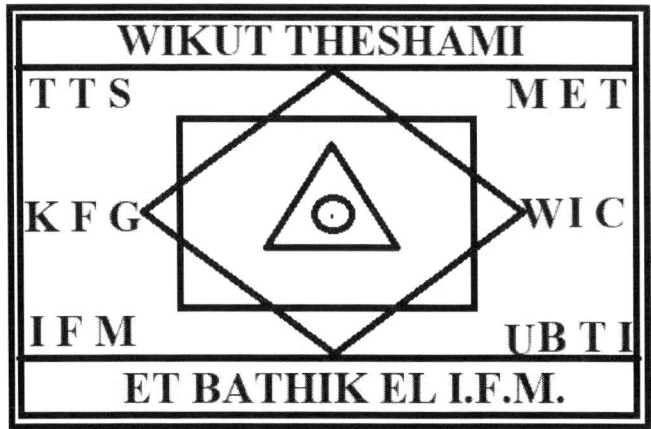

Make the above seal on clean parchment and pray the psalm over it three times in honor of the Most Holy Trinity, and anoint it with your own tears. Then sprinkle it with powdered myrrh and burn the seal outside.

PSALM 57

TO SURROUND A PERSON WITH ENEMIES

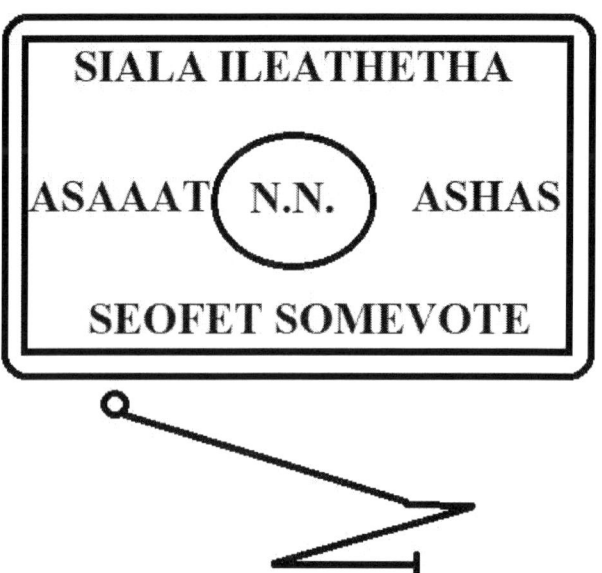

Make the above seal in ink made from rust and stormwater, with the character below it on the back. Replace N.N. with the name of the person on whom you are working. Pray the psalm 9 times over it on a Saturday when the moon is in it's dark half. Then hide the seal near the person's home or place of work.

FOR LOYALTY

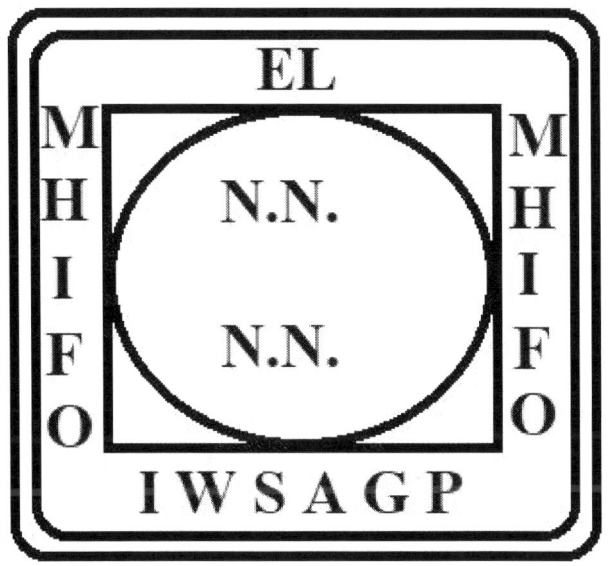

Make the above seal on clean parchment, the upper N.N. write your name, the lower N.N. the name of the person whom you wish to work on. It is best to write the seal in your own blood, but lacking that, red ink. Fumigate it with rose and frankincense, while praying the psalm seven times over it. Hide it in a clean place, a jewelry box being highly appropriate.

TO MAKE A PERSON AWAKE FROM SLEEP

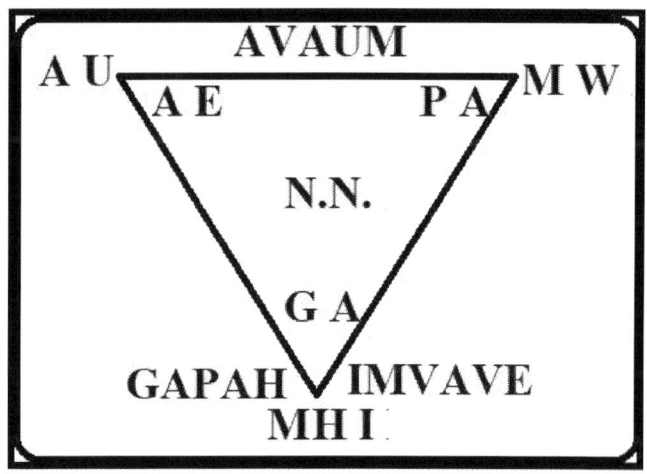

Mark the above seal on clean parchment, replacing N.N. with the person's name. Set a pot of water to boil with three spoons of olive oil added. Boil the seal while reciting the psalm five times.

TO TURN THE WORKS OF YOUR ENEMIES AGAINST THEM

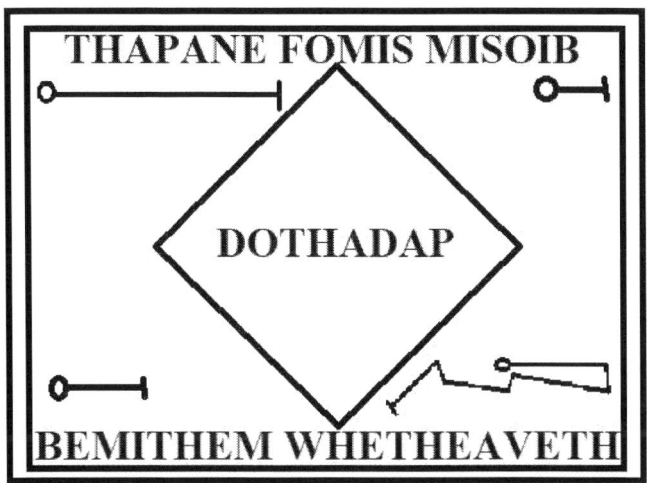

Make the above seal in black ink on a new mirror that has previously been washed seven times in a flowing river. Recite the psalm also seven times over it, and fumigate it with the leaves of an oak tree. Hang it on your wall, pointing toward the street, or direction of known enemies.

TO BE HONORED BY OTHERS

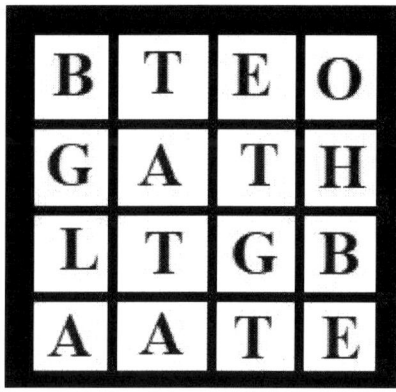

Make the above seal during the day and hour of Jupiter. Consecrated it with the psalm and fumigate it with white oak bark.

PSALM 58

TO INFLICT DENTAL PROBLEMS

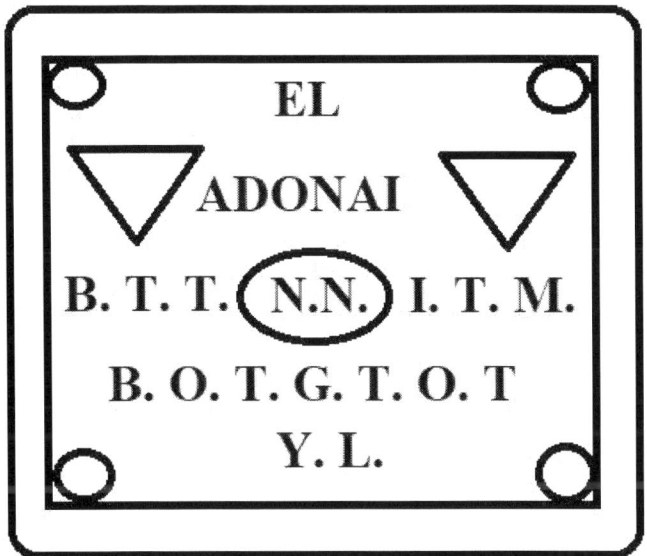

Make the above seal on lead, replacing N.N. with the name of the person on whom you are working. Fumigate it nine times with mullein and consecrate it with the psalm nine times as well. After this is complete, nail it, seal face inward, to the west side of a tree in a cemetery. The best time to do so would be the day and hour of Saturn when the moon is dark.

TO MAKE A PERSON'S WORDS UNTRUSTED

VV. VV. N. H. T. T. V. O. C. C. N. S. V.V.
VV. VV. N. H. T. T. V. O. C. C. N. S. V.V.
VV. VV. N. H. T. T. V. O. C. C. N. S. V.V.

Make the above seal on rusted metal with black ink. On the back, write the name and birthdate of the person you are charming. Fumigate it with myrrh and recite the psalm three times over it. Then hang it from a black cord from the west side of a tree in the cemetery.

PSALM 59

TO PUNISH TRAITORS AND REVEAL THEM

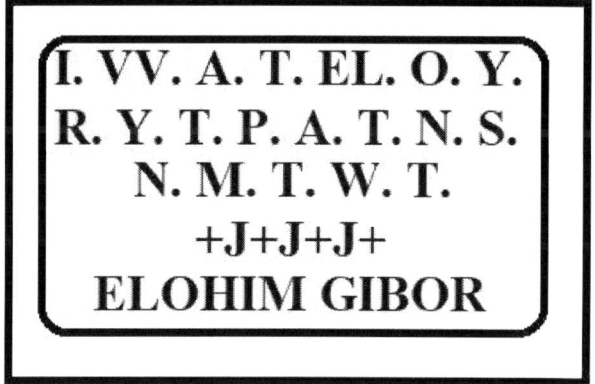

Make the above seal on clean parchment with black ink. Submerge it in a lamp of olive oil on a Tuesday at midnight. Recite the psalm 3 times in honor of the Most Holy Trinity and those who betray you will be punished in such a way that you will know who the traitors are by the misfortune that befalls them.

TO MAKE DOGS ATTACK A PERSON

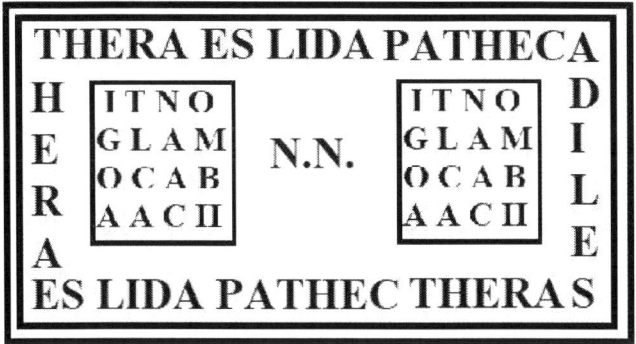

Copy the seal on clean parchment with iron gall ink. Replace N.N. with the name of the person, and fold the seal, hiding it in a piece of meat. Feed it to a stray dog after praying the psalm nine times over the meat.

TO REVEAL GOSSIP

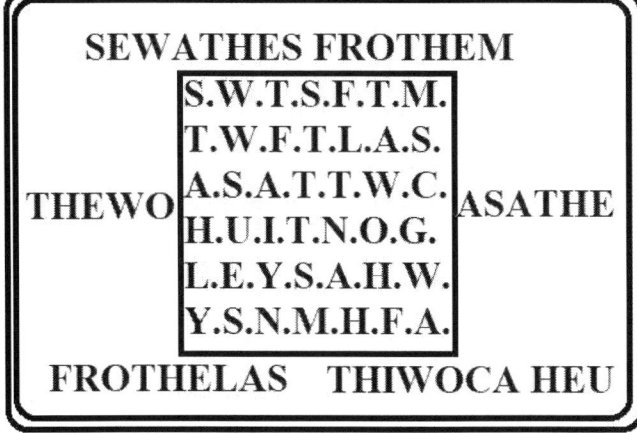

Should you wish a gossiper to get caught and the target of their gossip to hear what they say, mark the above seal. On the back, write the name of the gossiper, with three **+'s** over the name. Recite the psalm six times over the seal, and hang it from a tree by a single black thread.

TO MAKE SOMEONE A LAUGHING STOCK

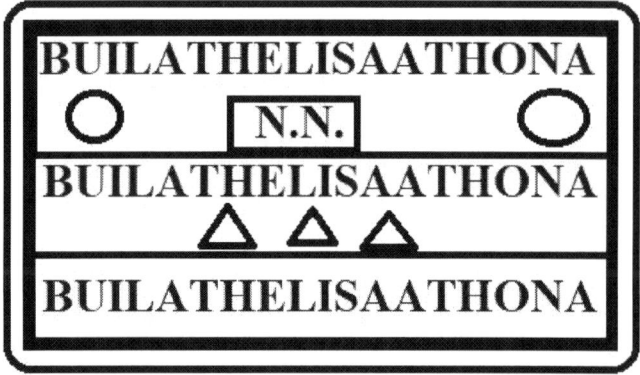

Mark the above seal on a new piece of white cloth. Replace the N.N. with the target's name. Recite the psalm over it three times in honor of the Most Holy Trinity, and tie it to a tree limb at a crossroads.

TO MAKE SOMEONE WHINE AND COMPLAIN

```
              T.W.A.F.F.A.H.I.N.S.

        INO  <  N.N.  >  SA

              THEWAV VOVOAH
```

Write the seal in black ink on a river rock. Replace the N.N. with the person's name and consecrate it by praying the psalm five times over the rock. Take the rock back to the place you retrieved it from, and lay it back in the water, seal side down.

PSALM 60

TO DESTROY A PERSON'S PROPERTY

```
            THELATIO
      ┌───┬───┬───┐
    I │ I │ H │ S │ T   V
    H │ L │ A │ T │ I   I
    A │ O │ M │ I │ F   I
    S │ F │ I │ I │ Q   S
      └───┴───┴───┘     Q
             MEIV
```

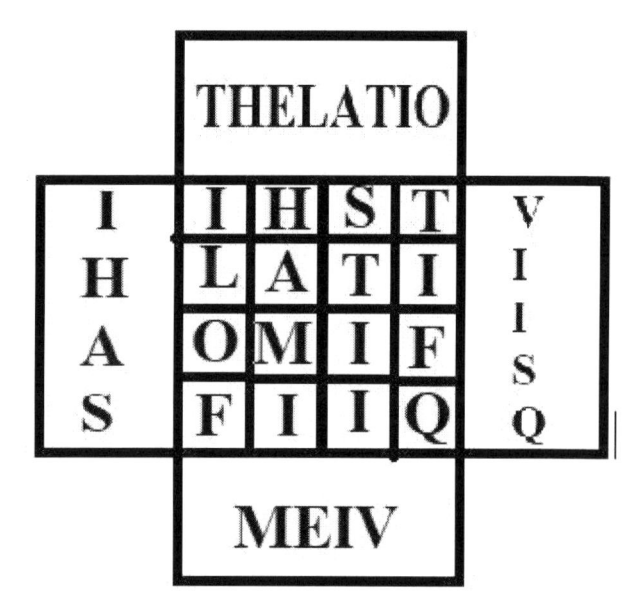

Mark the above seal on lead and pray the psalm over it nine times. Do this on a Saturday when the moon is dark, and bury it also on a Saturday when the moon is dark on the property.

FOR VICTORY

Every day for nine days, pray the psalm nine times over the ink you will use to create the seal. After the ink has been consecrated in this fashion, mark out the seal, and within the X place a drop of your own blood and carry it with you in a small vial of olive oil.

PSALM 61

TO CALL SOMEONE TO YOU

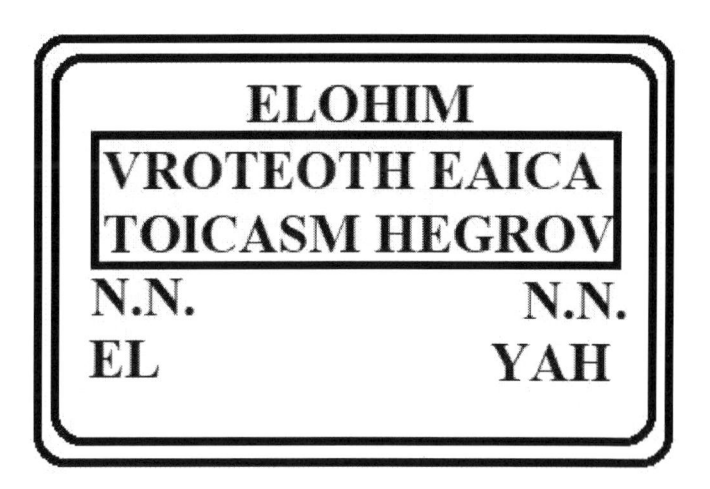

```
┌─────────────────────────────┐
│      ELOHIM                 │
│  ┌───────────────────────┐  │
│  │ VROTEOTH EAICA        │  │
│  │ TOICASM HEGROV        │  │
│  └───────────────────────┘  │
│  N.N.              N.N.     │
│  EL                YAH      │
└─────────────────────────────┘
```

Make seven copies of the above seal on paper with red ink, replacing N.N. with your name and the person whom you are calling.. Set a thurible with coals when the moon is increasing, and cast a seal in with some frankincense and recite the psalm. Repeat the procedure seven times, using up all the seals.

TO MAKE SOMEONE MOVE INTO YOUR HOME

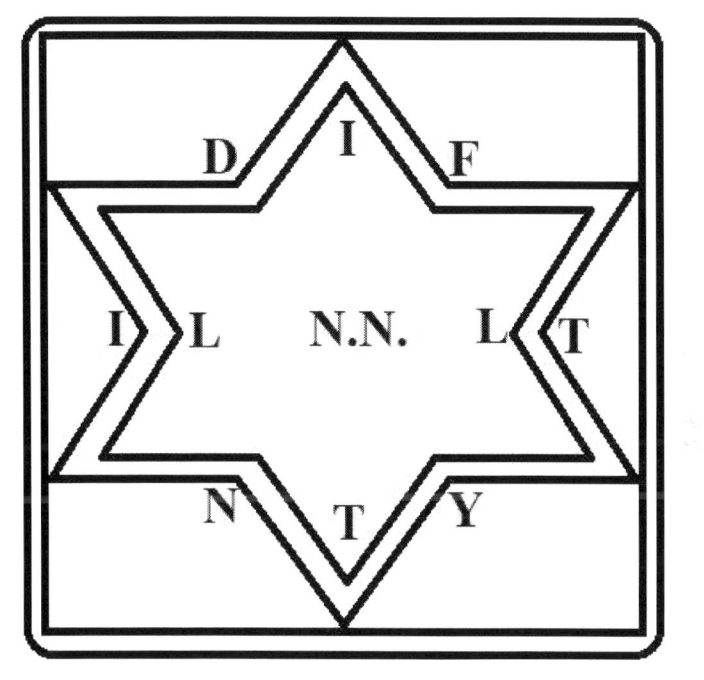

Mark the seal in green ink and replace the N.N. with the target's name. Pray the psalm over it seven times, and hide it near your front door.

TO MAKE A PERSON DEFEND YOU

Mark the above seal, replacing the top N.N. with your name, and the bottom N.N. with the target's name. Recite the psalm 12 times over it, fumigating it with cedar and myrrh. Carry it with you.

PSALM 62

FOR ANXIETY

Carve the above seal on dough and recite the psalm three times over it. Bake the bread then eat it.

TO MAKE TWO PEOPLE PLOT AGAINST EACH OTHER

```
         WIT MOTHE
   ┌─────────────────────┐
   │ I\               /I │
   │   \             /   │
   │    \   T       /    │
   │N.N. > B⋈H <  N.N.   │
   │    /   W       \    │
   │   /             \   │
   │ M/               \C │
   └─────────────────────┘
         BLEBIN THEACU
```

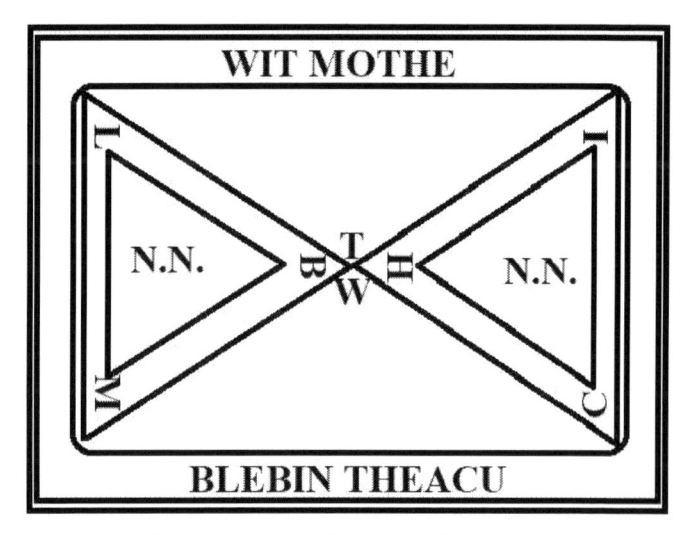

Mark the above seal on clean parchment and recite the psalm five times over it. Smear the seal in pig fat and leave it on a tombstone.

TO GAIN THE TRUST OF OTHERS

Carry this seal, consecrated with the psalm recited devoutly over it seven times. When you wish to use it, take it in your left hand, and blow three breaths over it, in the name of the Trinity, and place it in your left pocket.

TO DEVALUE THE MIGHTY

```
        L F
   U   T C R        N
       ┌─────┐
       │THABA│
       │LIWOA│
  G B O│BTANT│H E I
       │TAOAB│
       └─────┘
   A              Y
        W D
```

Mark the seal on lead and on the back, mark the name and birthdate of the target. Recite the psalm nine times over it on a Saturday during the dark of the moon, and nail it to the roots of a tree in the cemetery, on the western side.

PSALM 63

TO BRING TWO PEOPLE TOGETHER IN LOVE

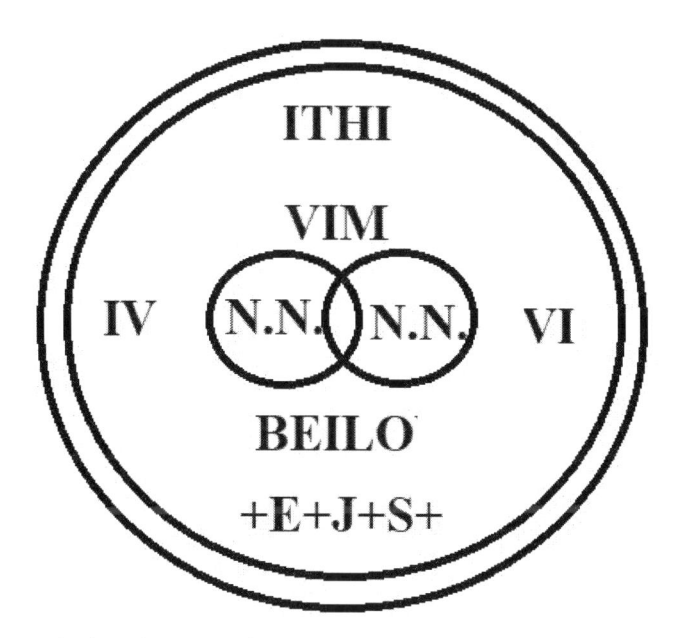

Mark the above seal on copper, during the day and hour of Venus, replacing the N.N. and N.N. with your name and the name of the target. Pray the psalm 7 times over it. This may be repeated as necessary, during the proper time. Wear the seal near your heart.

TO KINDLE PASSION AND DESIRE

```
        BEIO LIBETH
   M ┌─────────────┐ L
     │    N.N.     │
     │    N.N.     │
     │ ILIV  GIOU  │
     └──────I──────┘
```

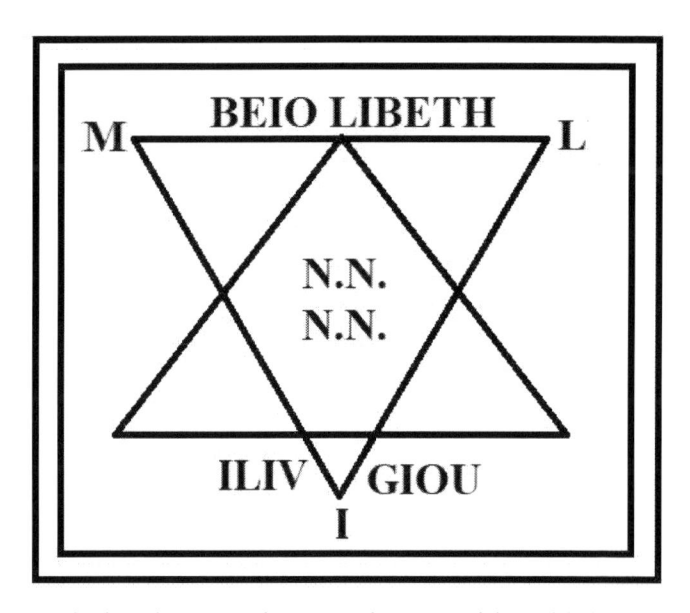

Mark the above seal on parchment with red ink. Recite the psalm seven times over it, and sew it up in green silk. Carry it on your person, near your genitals. Replace the N.N. and N.N. with your name and the name of your target.

TO MAKE A PERSON THINK OF YOU ALWAYS

Mark the above seal on a leaf of bay laurel. The empty spot within the fire is to be replaced by your initials and the target's initials. Recite the psalm seven times over it and burn the leaf to ashes. It is best if you can deposit them under the person's bed, but lacking that, anywhere they will come in contact with it.

FOR FIDELITY

I	C	T
Y	Y	R
H	U	M

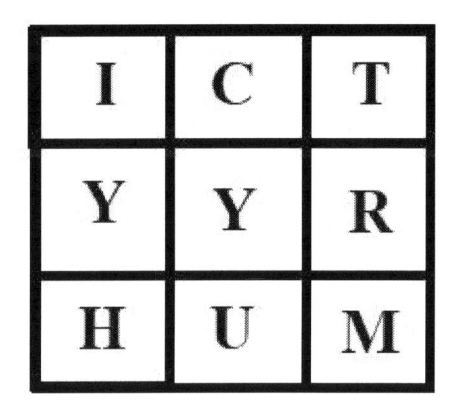

Mark the above seal on green cloth and wrap some of your hair and the hair of your partner's in it. Recite the psalm seven times over it, and keep the seal in a hidden place.

TO TURN AN ENEMY'S PLANS AGAINST THEM

```
        BEDESTHE
         CHIMEV
THOVEVTO    ⊗    THEDEOV
          THEA
         VIGODOTO
```

Mark the above seal on clean parchment with iron gall ink, with the enemy's name on the back. Recite the psalm five times over the seal and use an iron nail to drive it into the ground at a crossroads. This is best done on a Tuesday at midnight.

PSALM 64

AGAINST CONSPIRACIES

HIMEV THEKOTHEV UTHEPOE
HIMEV THEKOTHEV UTHEPOE
HIMEV THEKOTHEV UTHEPOE

Should enemies conspire against you, carry the above seal, consecrated with the psalm three times, in your left pocket.

TO STRIKE DOWN AN ENEMY

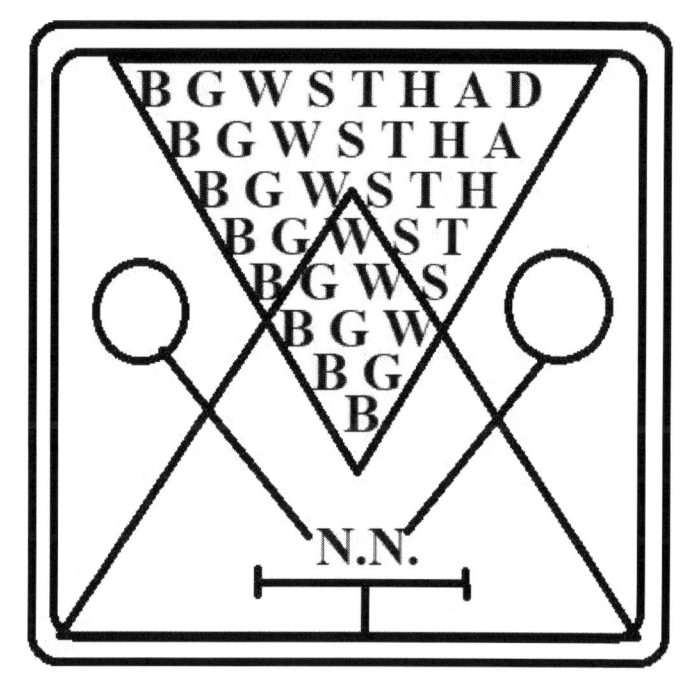

```
B G W S T H A D
B G W S T H A
B G W S T H
B G W S T
B G W S
B G W
B G
B

N.N.
```

Mark the above seal on leather in red ink, replacing the N.N. with the enemy's name. Daily, recite the psalm and drive a nail through the seal. When you finish with the seal, hang it on the gate of a cemetery.

TO EXPOSE GOSSIP AND SECRETS

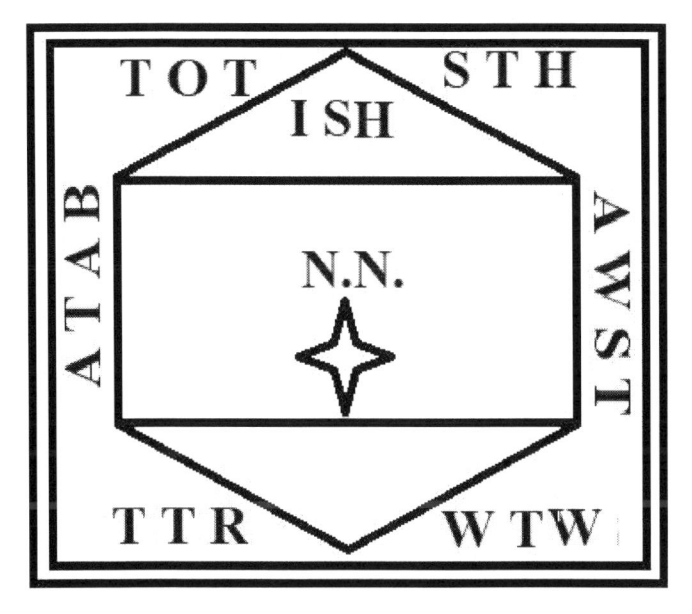

Mark the above seal on clean parchment in black ink, replacing N.N. with the name of the gossiper or person who holds the secret. Recite the psalm three times over it, and get a dog to lick the seal. Hide the seal where the person lives or works.

TO MAKE YOUR ENEMIES FEAR YOU

```
┌─────────────────────────────────┐
│   APEV VETHEV PROTHEV           │
│   ┌─────────────────────────┐   │
│   │ ╲         ╱ │            │
│   │   ╲  ___  ╱               │
│   │    ╳    ╳                 │
│   │   ╱  ‾‾‾  ╲               │
│   │ ╱         ╲ │            │
│   └─────────────────────────┘   │
│   HEHADO OV EL ANPOV            │
└─────────────────────────────────┘
```

Mark the above seal on clean parchment in red or black ink. Recite the psalm four times over it and burn it to ashes in the flame of an oil lamp. With the ashes, draw three crosses across your chest, and one on your tongue.

PSALM 65

FOR PROSPERITY IN THE HOME

```
         HEG
    VIT      IOU

       VEAV
       THIOV

       HOIHOTE
```

Mark the above seal on clean parchment or silver and consecrate it with the psalm twelve times. Anoint it with pure olive oil and hang it above your front door.

TO CALM A STORM AT SEA

```
WSTR
OTST
ROTW
```

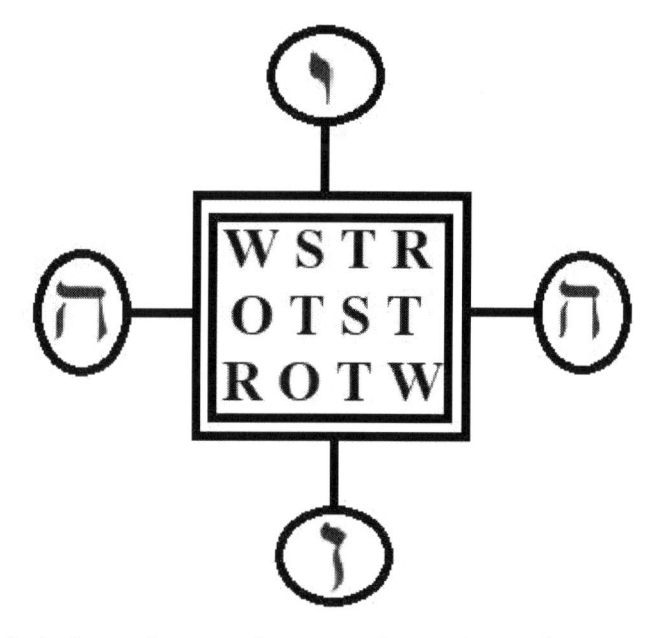

Mark the seal on parchment and pray the psalm over it three times in honor of the Most Holy Trinity and cast it into the waters.

FOR DROUGHT

```
     IOCAV
    THELAVI
     IOEIA
```

Mark the above seal and tie it to a fresh cut limb of willow. Place this in a jar of water outside under the sky and stir the water with it while praying the psalm three times.

FOR FOWL HUNTING

```
┌─────────────────────────┐
│        THEME            │
│   ┌───┬───┬───┐         │
│   │ T │A U│ H │         │
│   ├───┼───┼───┤         │
│   │ E │C I│ V │         │
│   ├───┼───┼───┤         │
│   │ M │E L│ O │         │
│   └───┴───┴───┘         │
│       AC UIVLO          │
└─────────────────────────┘
```

Make the above seal with ink and a feather quill pen, preferably of the same species you wish to hunt. Recite the psalm seven times over the seal, and attach it to your rifle when you go hunting.

PSALM 66

FOR DOMINATION

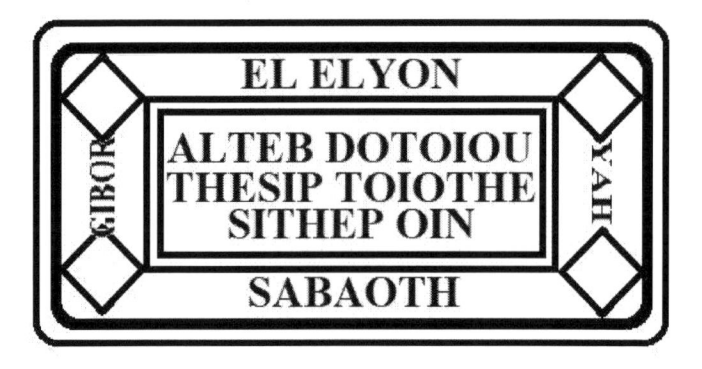

```
┌──────────────────────────────────┐
│           EL ELYON               │
│  ┌─┐  ALTEB DOTOIOU   ┌─┐        │
│  │G│  THESIP TOIOTHE  │Y│        │
│  │IBOR│ SITHEP OIN    │AH│       │
│  └─┘                  └─┘        │
│           SABAOTH                │
└──────────────────────────────────┘
```

Mark this seal on a strip of leather, in red ink, during a full moon on Tuesday. Pray the psalm over it five times, and sew the seal up into a piece of red cloth. Wear it from a cord around your neck.

TO END RAIN OR FLOOD

```
HET THESID LATHEP
   TOTHEV ONFO
     SHADDAI

MOSES            AARON
```

Mark the above seal in black ink on the bottom of a bowl. Pray the psalm nine times over it, and set it outside to catch the rain. When the rain has washed away the ink, turn the bowl upside down and leave it until the rain passes.

TO KEEP SOMEONE IN JAIL

Mark the above seal on a piece of lead, on a Saturday during the hour of Mars, using an iron nail as a stylus. Replace the N.N. with the name of the target and recite the psalm nine times over it. Afterwards, drive the nail directly into the center of the person's name, and bury it under a heavy rock by a thorn tree.

TO OPPRESS ALL ASPECTS OF A PERSON'S LIFE

```
         N.N.
    PRO OHIL
S   PRO OHI    S
A   PRO OH     A
B   PRO O      B
A   PRO        A
O   PR         O
T   P          T
H              H
```

Make ash by burning willow twigs and mix with storm water and clay to make an ink. Recite the psalm five times over the ink. It is preferred to make the ink on a Friday at 3:00pm.

The seal is to be made on an earthenware jar with a lid, on a Saturday at midnight. Replace N.N. with the name of your target.

After the jar has been made, you must find seven dead creatures such as frogs, toads, reptiles of any sort, or spiders. They must have already been killed by any hand but your own.

Over each animal, whisper the psalm and the name of the person whom you are working, then placing the creature within the jar. After this has been done over each creature, the target's name is whisper three times into the jar, then it is sealed with wax. The jar is then buried in the grave of a person who has died violently.

TO MAKE A PERSON COME PAY THEIR DEBT

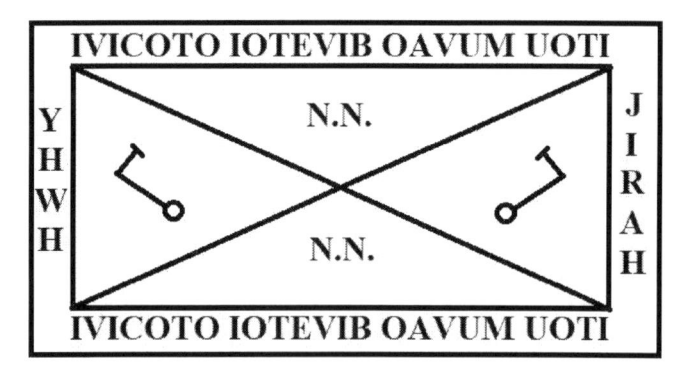

```
┌─────────────────────────────────────┐
│    IVICOTO IOTEVIB OAVUM UOTI       │
├──┬───────────────────────────────┬──┤
│Y │         N.N.                  │ J│
│H │    ╲               ╱          │ I│
│W │     ╲             ╱           │ R│
│H │      ╳           ╳            │ A│
│  │         N.N.                  │ H│
├──┴───────────────────────────────┴──┤
│    IVICOTO IOTEVIB OAVUM UOTI       │
└─────────────────────────────────────┘
```

Mark the above seal on a clean piece of parchment in green ink over which three Hail Marys have been said. Replace the top N.N. with your name, and the bottom N.N. with the name of the debtor. Recite the psalm seven times over the seal, and place it within your left shoe.

SO THAT A PERSON WILL GIVE YOU GIFTS

(Seal: a triangle within a double circle, containing the words FATIA, AOORI, IWS, and WOBAG)

Draw the above seal on a small piece of parchment in your own blood. Recite the psalm seven times over it and when you go to meet the person, endeavor to touch the psalm to your hand, write the words written on it, and touch your hand to the person. Thereafter, they will be impelled to give things to you.

TO MAKE A PERSON SPEAK TO YOU

C	A	H
A	Y	W
F	E	E

Write the above square on clean parchment and hold it in your mouth while praying the psalm three times, after each recitation stating the person's full name. Then swallow the seal.

PSALM 67

FOR JUSTICE

Write the psalm on birch bark, replacing N.N. and N.N. with the individuals who are having a legal dispute. Pray the psalm over it four times, and nine times the Lord's Prayer. Thus, justice will be done, regardless of personal opinions.

FOR ADVICE

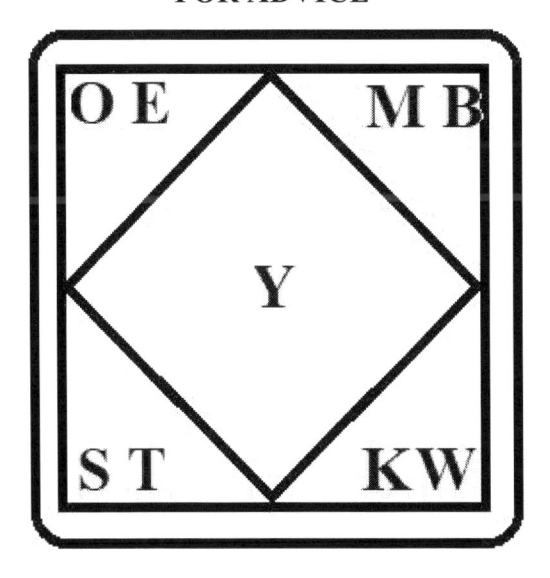

```
O E         M B
     \   /
      \ /
   ---- Y ----
      / \
     /   \
S T         K W
```

Mark the above seal on clean parchment in red ink and pray the psalm over it three times in honor of the Most Holy Trinity. On the back, write the question or matter on which you seek advice. Burn the seal to ashes, and mark a cross on your forehead with it. Do this before bed, and the answer will come to you in a dream.

PSALM 68

TO DRIVE SOMEONE AWAY

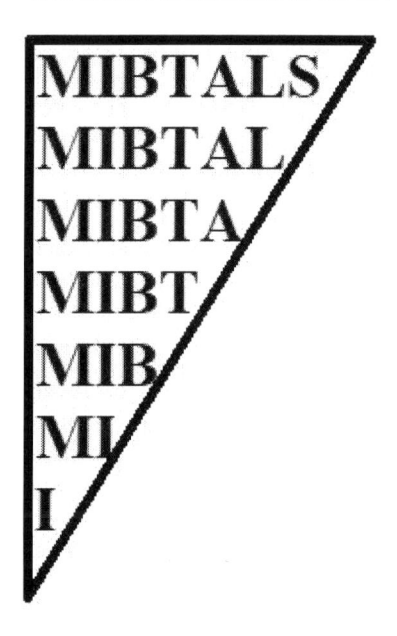

```
MIBTALS
MIBTAL
MIBTA
MIBT
MIB
MI
I
```

Make the above seal on parchment in black ink and recite the psalm over it three times. Burn the triangle to ashes, and sprinkle the ashes on the person, their seat, doorway, etc.

FOR SINGLE MOTHERS TO FIND HUSBANDS

```
┌─────────────────────────────┐
│           AAT               │
│  ┌───────────────────────┐  │
│  │ AV TOTHEV ADEO VV.    │  │
│  └───────────────────────┘  │
│  DOW                   TFA  │
└─────────────────────────────┘
```

Mark the above seal on copper and pray the psalm over it seven times, starting on a Friday, every day until the next Friday. When not being prayed over, keep it within your Bible. After your days have been completed, wear it around your neck with faith.

TO INSPIRE FRIENDSHIP

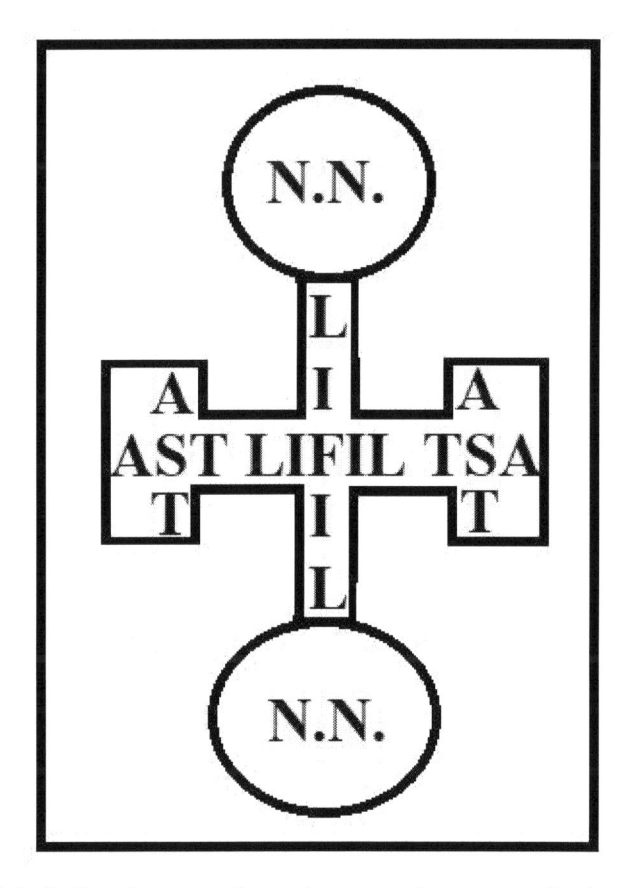

Mark the above seal on clean parchment, replacing the top N.N. with your name, and the bottom N.N. with the name of the target. Pray the psalm six times over the seal on a Monday between dawn and noon, while facing the east. Then wear the seal near your heart.

TO FIND A HOME

Make the above seal on a smooth stone in black ink, place it in a bowl of olive oil, and pray the psalm daily over it every day for nine days. After each recitation, mark a cross on both of your palms with the oil. When the house is found, bury the bowl in the yard.

FOR A MAN TO OBTAIN THE ATTENTION OF WOMEN

A	Y	A	T
W	A	T	W
W	P	I	A
A	M	T	F

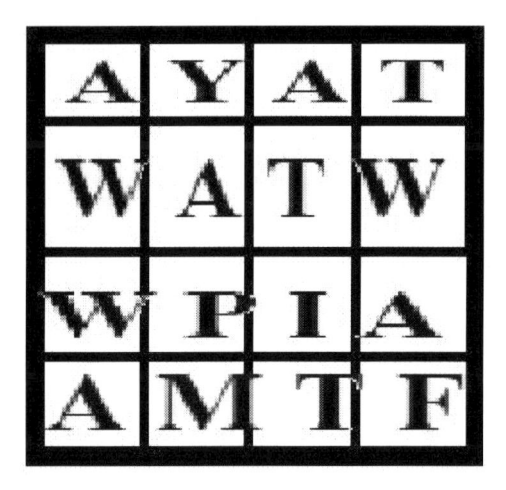

Pray the psalm seven times over green ink and draw the square on clean parchment. Carry the seal, sewn up in green silk, near your left testicle.

PSALM 69

TO PREVENT DROWNING

```
SAMIOG    HAKUT

    JAH

OMIN     VOTEV
```

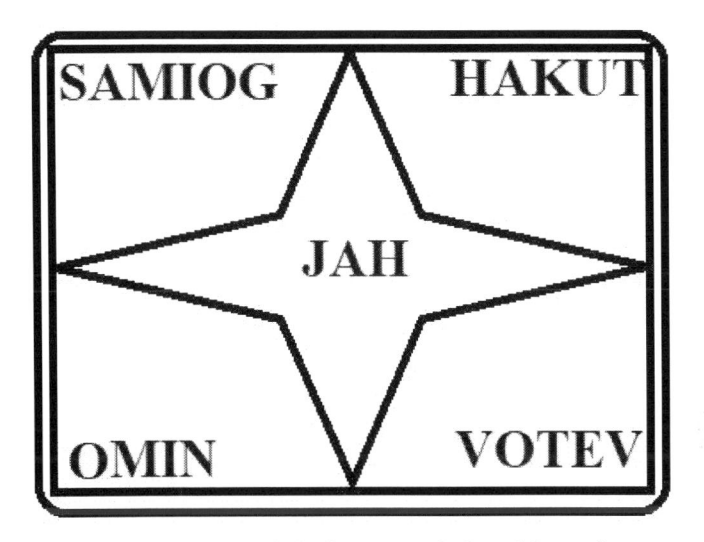

Carry the above seal tied to your left ankle and consecrated with the psalm seven times, in honor of the Seven Spirits that minister around the Throne of the Almighty.

TO MAKE THE INNOCENT SEEM GUILTY

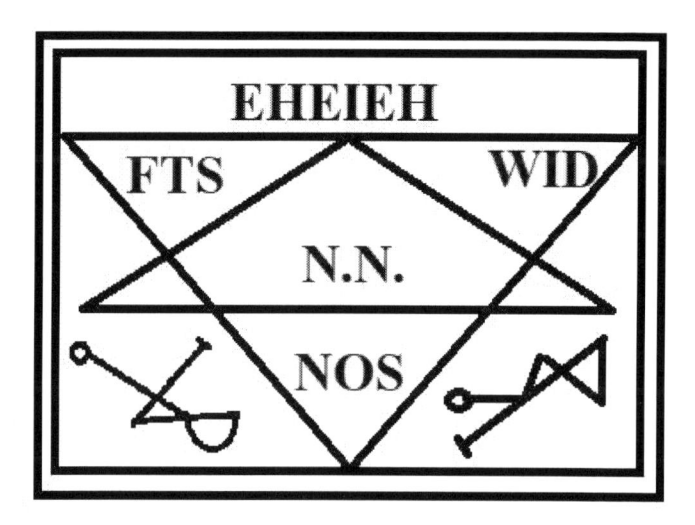

Draw the seal on a piece of broken pottery in black ink and pray the psalm over it nine times during the dark half of the moon on a Saturday. Replace N.N. with the target's name, and afterwards leave it on a tombstone.

TO MAKE A PERSON FOOLISH

```
         ILO FEM

       IA KMF
        N.N.
      IOGO QOM F.

         VOD GO
```

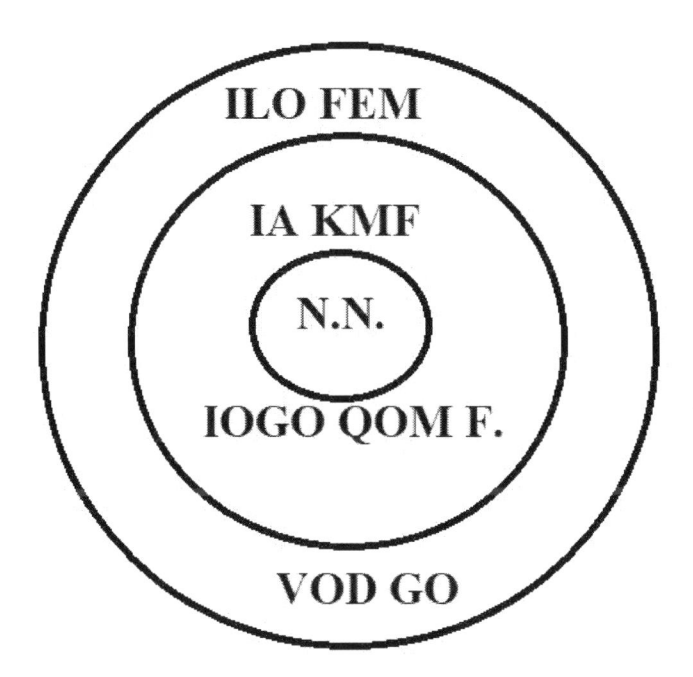

Mark the seal on parchment in black ink, replacing N.N. with the person's name. Pray the psalm four times over it, and lay it on a plate. On top of the seal, place an amount of seed and grain, and leave it under a tree for birds to peck at.

TO TURN SIBLINGS AGAINST EACH OTHER

```
┌─────────────────────────────┐
│      AF TOMO FAS            │
│   ┌─────────────────┐       │
│   │    EHEIEH .     │       │
│   └─────────────────┘       │
│      TOMO MOCH              │
└─────────────────────────────┘
```

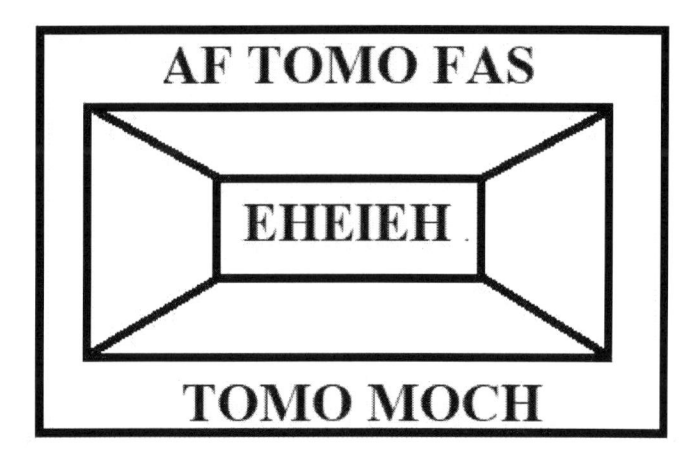

Mark the above seal on parchment in red ink. On the back, write the names of the siblings. Take an egg, and break a small hole in it, placing the seal within. Pray the psalm over it five times, and throw it onto the roof of the family home, or the home of one of the siblings in particular.

PSALM 70

TO RUIN ALL PLOTS AGAINST YOU

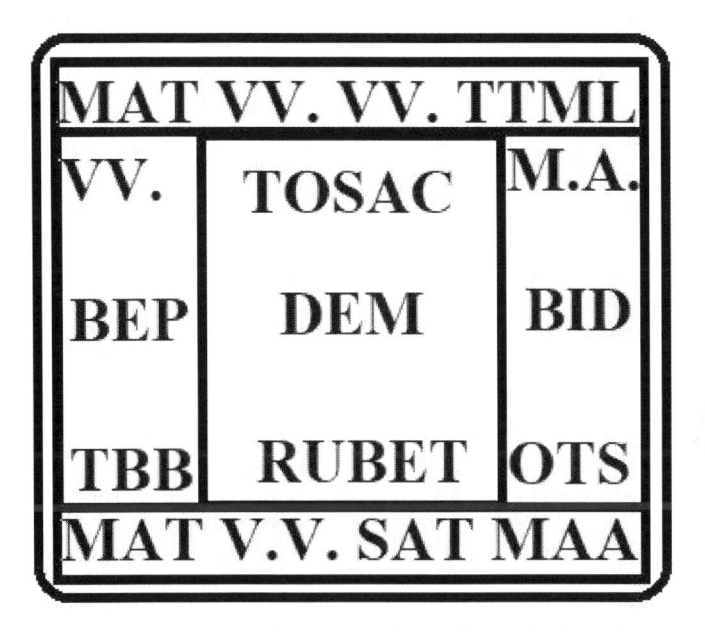

```
┌─────────────────────────────┐
│  MAT VV. VV. TTML           │
├─────┬───────────────┬───────┤
│ VV. │    TOSAC      │ M.A.  │
│     │               │       │
│ BEP │    DEM        │ BID   │
│     │               │       │
│ TBB │    RUBET      │ OTS   │
├─────┴───────────────┴───────┤
│  MAT V.V. SAT MAA           │
└─────────────────────────────┘
```

Carry the above seal engraved on silver during the full moon and consecrated with the psalm seven times.

TO BE ADMIRED BY OTHERS

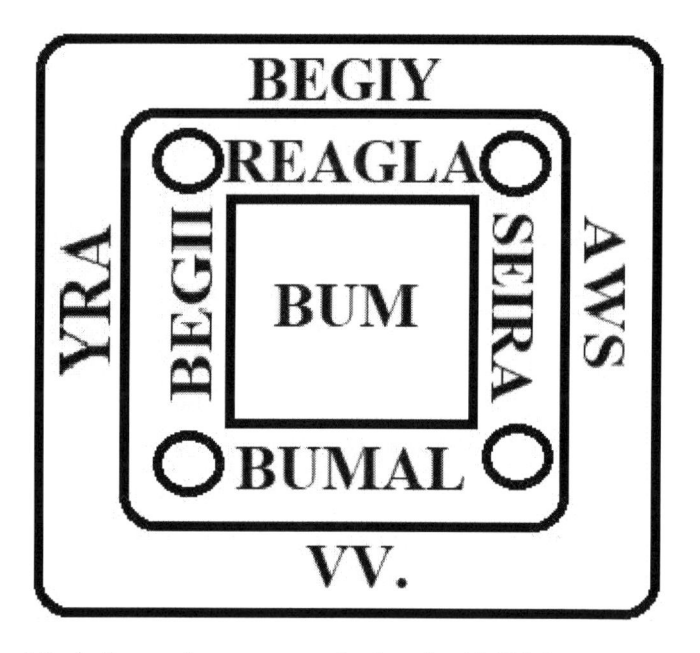

Mark the seal on copper during the Full Moon on a Friday and anoint it with oil of roses seven times, praying the psalm over it seven times during the process. Carry the seal with you.

PSALM 71

FOR CHILDBIRTH

```
IOBRO MEF FMMW
IB                    MIV
  Y.B.M.F.F.M.M.W.
MEV                   FEM
IOBRO MEF FMMW
```

Mark the seal on clean parchment in blue ink and lay it over the womb of the mother and pray the psalm three times over the seal, as it lay on the mother's womb. This will assist in having a safe delivery.

TO MAKE A PERSON PRAISE YOU

```
MMI FWI PDI SADL
MIMIV WIP DEIS ADAL
M I F W Y P D S A L
```

Write the seal on clean parchment in amber ink. On the back, write the name and birthdate of the person you are enchanting. Hold the seal against your throat and recite the psalm, facing south, seven times. Do this daily for three days.

FOR MARITAL FIDELITY
E.VV.EHEIEH.O.A.G. D.N.F.M.

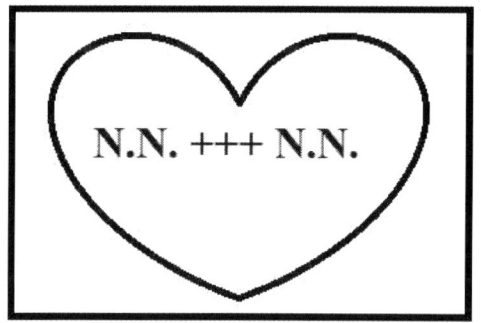

```
┌─────────────────────────┐
│         ♡               │
│     N.N. +++ N.N.       │
│                         │
└─────────────────────────┘
```

E.VV.EHEIEH.O.A.G. D.N.F.M.

Mark the above seal on copper, replacing N.N. and N.N. with your name and your spouse's name. This is best done on the day and hour of Venus, with Venus well aspected. Recite the psalm seven times over it and fumigate it with Venusian herbs. Afterwards, keep the seal hidden in a bible in a safe and clean place.

TO ENCHANT A RECALCITRANT LOVER

Y.VV. IMH A.C.M. OM +++

Mark the above seal on clean parchment in red ink and pray the psalm over it three times in honor of the Most Holy Trinity, while facing East, at sunrise on a Friday. Burn the seal to ashes, and secret them into his food or drink

PSALM 72

FOR PROSPERITY

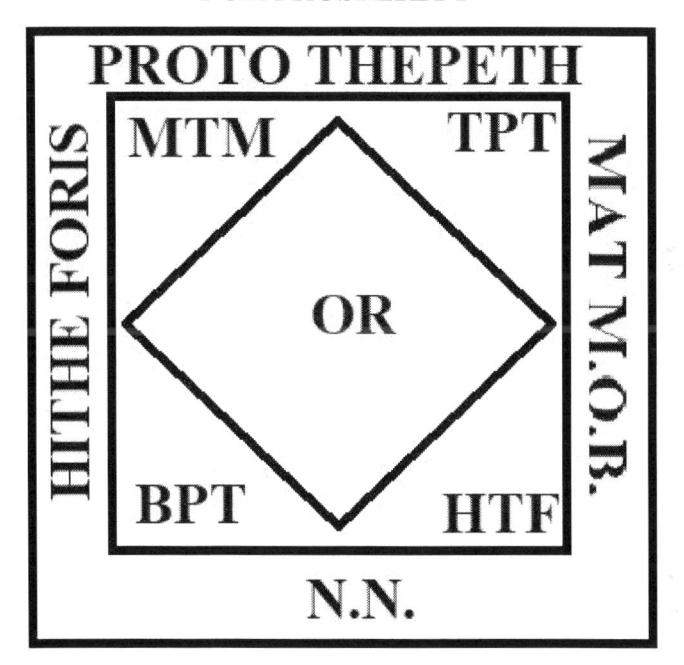

```
┌─────────────────────────────┐
│      PROTO THEPETH          │
│   MTM           TPT         │
│ H                      M    │
│ I        ◇             A    │
│ T                      T    │
│ H       OR             M.   │
│ E                      O.   │
│ F                      B.   │
│ O        ◇                  │
│ R                           │
│ I  BPT           HTF        │
│ S       N.N.                │
└─────────────────────────────┘
```

Make the above seal on cloth with golden or amber ink, and attach it to a stick of white oak, severed on a Thursday at sunrise, to make a flag. Plant this on a high hill or mountain, replacing N.N. with your own name, and pray the psalm three times to each of the directions.

FOR MATERIAL WEALTH

```
        FHA   AL   FSB
           GIHIM
           BLEHIM
           MAPEP
        DAL        MAG
```

Carve the seal onto a brass plate and recite the psalm over it seven times. In the center of the plate, set an oil lamp to burn and daily light the lamp and recite the psalm three times.

PSALM 73

FOR RECOVERY OF HEALTH

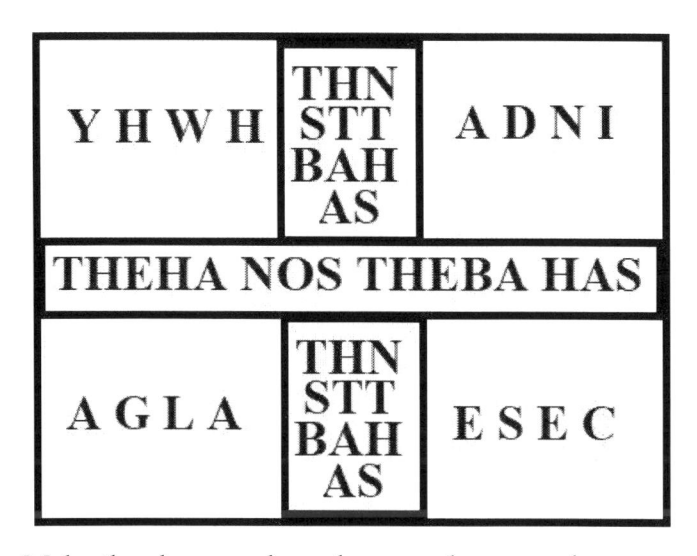

YHWH	THN STT BAH AS	ADNI
THEHA NOS THEBA HAS		
AGLA	THN STT BAH AS	ESEC

Make the above seal on clean parchment and pray the psalm five times over it and fumigate it with frankincense and myrrh. Place the seal under the mattress of the ill person.

TO MAKE A PERSON GRIEVE

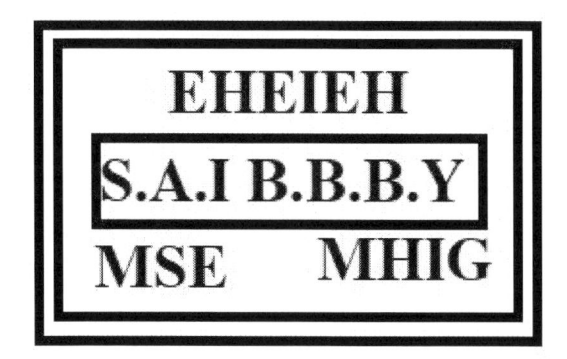

```
EHEIEH
S.A.I B.B.B.Y
MSE        MHIG
```

Mark the seal on clean parchment with the name of the target on the back. Pray the psalm three times over it, and place it within the mouth of a dead fish. Draw a hook through the mouth of the fish, and hang it from the limbs of a tree in a high place, far from water.

татко MAKE A PERSON FOLLOW AFTER YOU

Triangle seal containing:
Y. EHEIEH
N.N.
AWY YHM BM RH

Mark the seal on copper, replacing N.N. with the name of the person. Do this on a Friday during the Hour of Venus, and fumigate the seal with myrtle while reciting the psalm seven times. Wear it below the waist.

PSALM 74

TO DESTROY AN ENEMY

```
┌─────────────────────────────────┐
│   . T.I.F.T.F.O.Y.G.A.D.T. .    │
│  ┌──────────────────────────┐   │
│T │   TAIV  ╱╲   OIG         │ T │
│.I│        ╱  ╲              │.I.│
│F │       ╱    ╲             │ F │
│T │      ╱      ╲            │ T │
│.F│     ╱        ╲           │.F.│
│O │    ╱   N.N.   ╲          │ O │
│.Y│    ╲          ╱          │.Y.│
│G │     ╲        ╱           │ G │
│.A│      ╲      ╱            │.A.│
│D │       ╲    ╱             │ D │
│.T│   THEV ╲  ╱ ADEST        │.T.│
│  └──────────────────────────┘   │
│   . T.I.F.T.F.O.Y.G.A.D.T. .    │
└─────────────────────────────────┘
```

Mark the above seal on parchment in iron gall ink. Replace N.N. with the name of the target. Recite the psalm nine times over it, fumigating the seal with sulfur. Wrap the seal in a canine's tooth, and bury it in the grave of a small child.

TO BRING DOWN A POWERFUL FOE

Mark the above seal on lead, with an iron nail, during the dark of the moon on a Saturday, replacing N.N. with the name of the enemy. Recite the psalm nine times over the seal, and lay it with the bones of a fish within a wicker basket. Bury the basket at the edge of running water.

TO WARD A PLACE

IVIV SATHEB OTE

On four rods of cedar, carve the above words and stain them with a drop of your own blood. Recite the psalm three times over each rode. Bury them, pointing vertically, at the four corners of the property.

PSALM 75

PROTECTION DURING EARTHQUAKES

W	T	E	A
A	I	P	Q
I	I	I	W
H	I	P	F

Mark the above square on a brass plate and consecrate it by fumigating it with myrrh and reciting the psalm seven times. Hang the plate on the wall of your dining room.

TO CAUSE STOMACH ILLNESS

```
ITH O ADNI IAC
     EDI
   EL PIO
 DTI    VD
  AAT WOT
```

Mark the seal on clean parchment and pray the psalm nine times over it. Burn the seal to ashes, and sprinkle a pinch in the person's food or drink.

PSALM 76

FOR PEACE IN THE HOME

PAX

H T I I S

Mark this seal on silver, consecrating it with the psalm three times and fumigating it with camphor. Whenever food is prepared in the home, strive to touch the seal to each person's food, that peace will enter through it.

FOR CHARM AND ATTRACTION

IAR W.L.M. MATHAM R.W.G.

Write these words in cherry juice on a white plate. Pray the psalm seven times over it, and pour three teaspoons of holy water onto the plate, dissolving the words. Drink the liquid.

TO INFLUENCE RACES

A Y R E O Y B H A C L S
A Y R E O Y B H A C L
A Y R E O Y B H A C
A Y R E O Y B H A
A Y R E O Y B H
A Y R E O Y B
A Y R E O Y
A Y R E O
A Y R E
A Y R
A Y
A

Mark the above seal on clean parchment in grey ink and recite the psalm four times over it. Should you wish to use it on a horse, car, or person; hold it in your left hand and say their name three times, and they will fall behind in the race.

PSALM 77

FOR EYESIGHT

```
         YOCHEM / EFROCH
              N.N.
         Y K        M E
              F C
```

Mark the seal during the full moon on silver and pray the psalm three times over it. Touch the seal to your eyes daily, and pray the Lord's prayer three times, the Hail Mary three times, and the Gloria three times.

TO SILENCE A PERSON

```
╔═══════════════════════════╗
║      IWAT AST             ║
║   ┌───────────────┐       ║
║   │   IWT TTS     │       ║
║   │    N.N.       │       ║
║   │               │       ║
║   │   IWT TTS     │       ║
║   └───────────────┘       ║
║     OTROU TOS AK          ║
╚═══════════════════════════╝
```

Mark the seal on clean parchment and replace N.N. with the name of the person. Recite the psalm nine times over the seal, fumigating it with sulfur. Bind it with cord, and bury it in the grave of a child that never drew breath.

TO CALL A STORM

```
          YAR
    T.H.R. / \ A.F.B.
THEHE <       > REWITH
    .W.T.Y. \ / F.A.F
         FLABAN
```

Mark the above seal on parchment with iron gall ink. Recite the psalm five times over it. Burn it outdoors on a small fire composed of twigs from nine different oaks.

PSALM 78

TO SPEAK WITH THE SPIRIT OF AN ANCESTOR

```
        I.W.U.      F.O.O.
            H.A.K.
         ( circle )
        T.O.A.    H.T.U.
        .H.T.T.    T.W.H.
```

Write the above seal on a white plate in black ink and pray the psalm nine times over it, fumigating it with dittany of crete. Within the circle, write your question and place a bowl of water over it. Place a candle or lamp within the water, sticking out, and light it. Go to sleep and the spirit will answer your question in a dream. Afterwards, the seal must be washed completely off, and the water thrown out of the home into the street.

PROTECTION FROM BULLETS

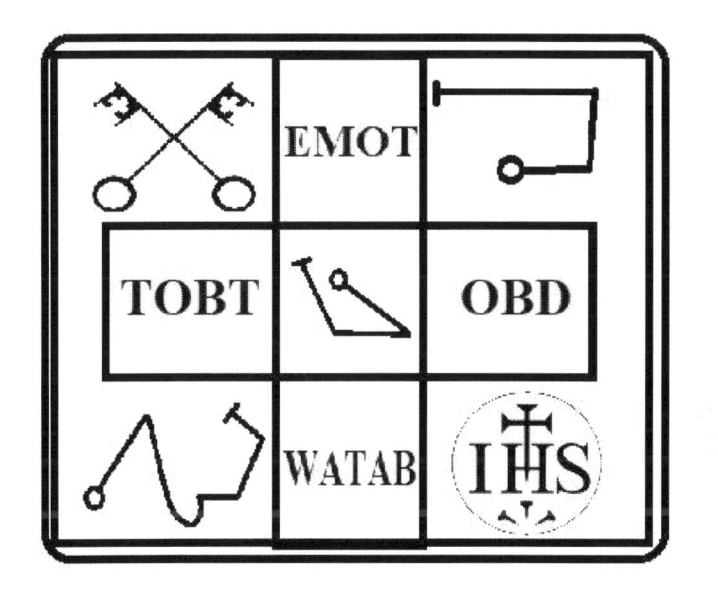

Mark the above seal on lead with an iron nail on a Saturday during the hour of Mars, and pray the psalm nine times over it. Anoint it with myrrh oil and sew it up in black cloth. Wear it on your person. (Lead is hazardous)

TO OPEN PATHS OF OPPORTUNITY

```
        GATHE
        TRIT
WIA─           ─HES
        ATES
        WASA
```

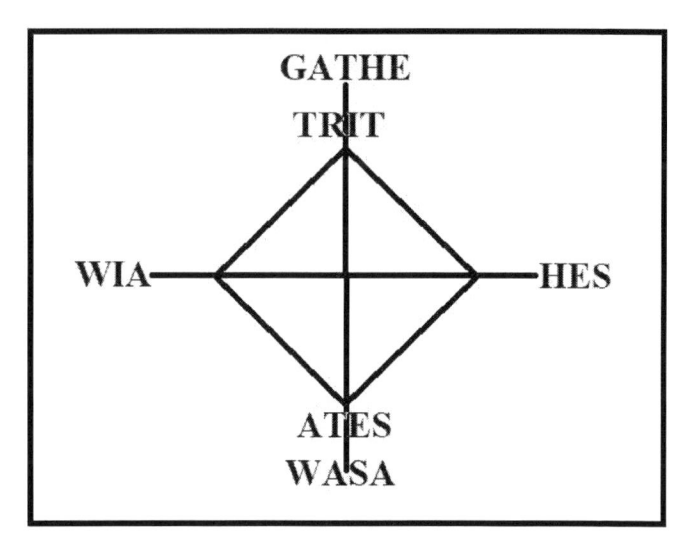

Take pure white chalk to a Mass, and dip it in the holy water. When the priest gives the benediction, whisper the words of the seal over the chalk.

Take the same chalk and draw the seal on the inside of your door, and pray the psalm over it three times. Do this for three days. After the three days, use your palms to wipe away the image, and then wipe the chalk dust across your face.

TO CALM ANGER

```
TATHRHAADNSUHFW
TATIIRIIAADNSUIIF
TATIIRIIAADNSUII
TATHRHAADNSU
TATHRHAADNS
TATHRHAADN
TATHRHAAD
TATHRHAA
TATHRHA
TATIIRII
TATHR
TATH
TAT
TA
T
```

Mark the above seal on clean parchment in our own blood. Recite the psalm four times over it and reduce it to ashes. Sprinkle the ashes in the person's food.

TO TURN PEOPLE AGAINST A PERSON

```
┌─────────────────────┐
│    HITWA            │
│   REAHIT            │
│   ◇ N.N. ◇          │
│    WAG              │
│   HOTHE             │
└─────────────────────┘
```

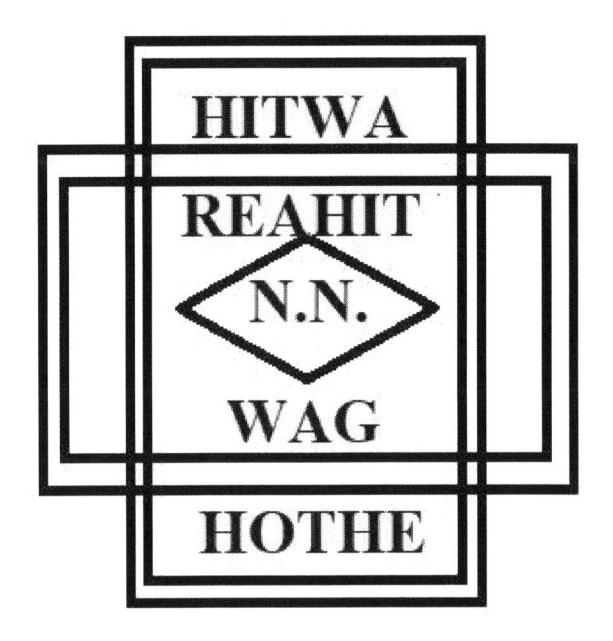

Carve the above seal on bread dough, using a thorn, replacing N.N. with the name of the person. Bake the bread until it is hard, but not burned.

Recite the psalm five times over the bread, and soak it in a bowl of goat's milk. After three days, throw it over the gate to the cemetery.

PSALM 79

TO CAUSE HEMORRHAGE

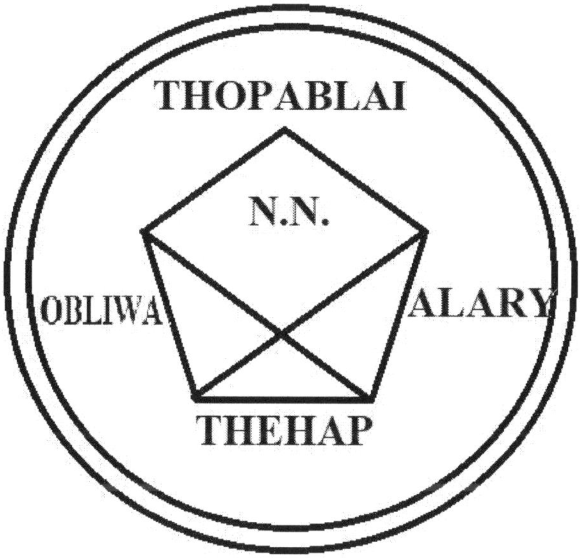
THOPABLAI
N.N.
OBLIWA
ALARY
THEHAP

Mark the above seal on clean paper with black ink, replacing N.N. with the name of the target. Recite the psalm nine times, in between each recitation, reciting the person's name, and the words upon the seal. After this has been accomplished, wrap the seal in raw meat, and leave it in a place visited by carrion birds.

TO RETURN EVIL

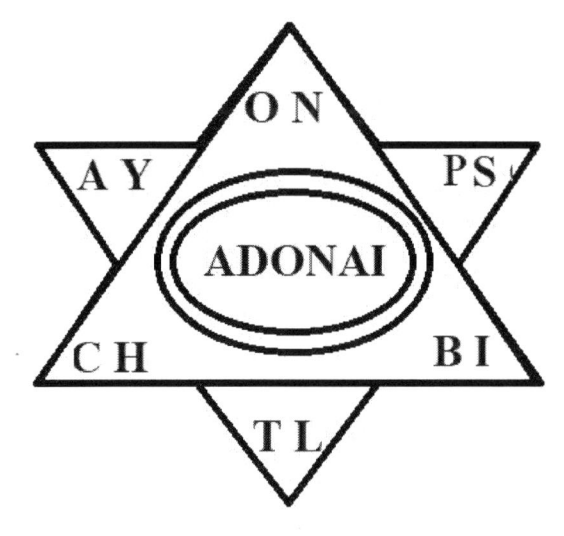

If a person is committing acts to harm you, submerge the above seal in the oil of a lamp and light it at midnight on a Tuesday and pray the psalm five times.

PSALM 80

TO INFLICT SADNESS

Draw the above seal on a small mirror in black ink, and after the ink has dried, cover it with a black cloth and never look into the reflection again. Pray the psalm nine times over it, and endeavor to catch the reflection of your target in the mirror. Once you have done so, and even better if you can trick them into looking into it, cover it again with the cloth, and never allow the mirror to see light again.

TO MAKE A PLACE PRONE TO THEFT

```
BAFTRIO
TRIOBAF
IOBTRAF
FATROBI
ROBITAF
BITAFOR
```

Mark the above seal on aluminum, during the dark of the moon on a Wednesday. Fumigate it with coriander and pepper, and hide it on the property.

PSALM 81

TO DRIVE AWAY A MEDDLING PERSON FROM ANOTHER

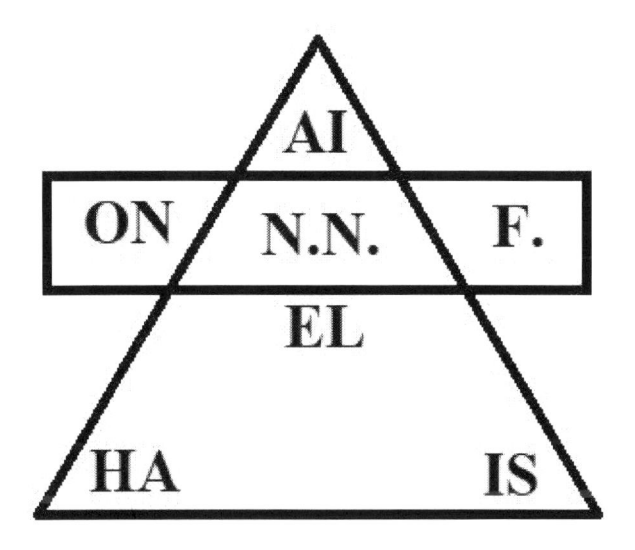

Mark the above seal on clean parchment, on a Sunday at noon with red ink, replacing N.N. with the name of the person you wish driven away. Pray the psalm three times over it, and reduce the seal to ashes. Mix the ashes in the food, and the one who eats it will not wish to have any dealings with the person whose name was written on the seal.

TO RECEIVE A SIGN FROM ABOVE

```
         IA
         TAO
    IA IA TAO IO IO
         TAO
          IO
```

Mark the sign on clean parchment in purple ink and pray the psalm over it seven times, while holding the seal in your left hand and concentrating on your question. Carry the seal on your person until the sign is given.

PSALM 82

TO CAUSE CONFUSION

```
┌─────────────────────────┐
│  ┌───────────────────┐  │
│  │      ELOHIM       │  │
│  │       ╱╲          │  │
│  │      ╱  ╲         │  │
│  │     ╱ K. ╲        │  │
│  │    ╱ ┌───┐╲       │  │
│  │   ╱T.│N.N│D.╲     │  │
│  │  ╱   └───┘   ╲    │  │
│  │ ╱     N.      ╲   │  │
│  │╱_____╲  │  │
│  │T.    WAIN    NUT  │  │
│  └───────────────────┘  │
└─────────────────────────┘
```

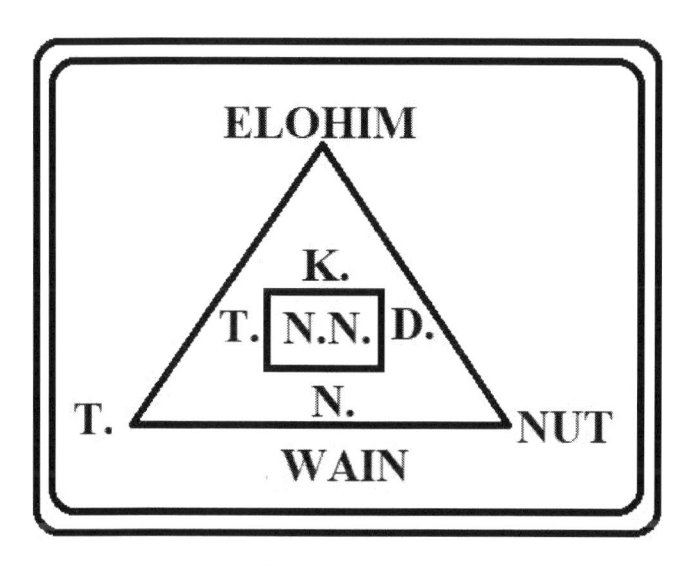

Mark the seal on unleavened dough, replacing N.N. with the target. Pray the psalm three times over it, and knead the dough into seven balls of dough. Place each one on top of a different anthill.

PSALM 83

TO MAKE A PERSON'S PRESENCE KNOWN

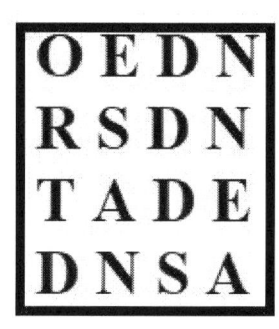

O	E	D	N
R	S	D	N
T	A	D	E
D	N	S	A

Mark the above seal on seven strips of palm and pray the psalm three times over each square. Afterwards, cast them on to smouldering frankincense and allow the smoke to drift into the open air.

TO WASTE SOMEONE'S HEALTH

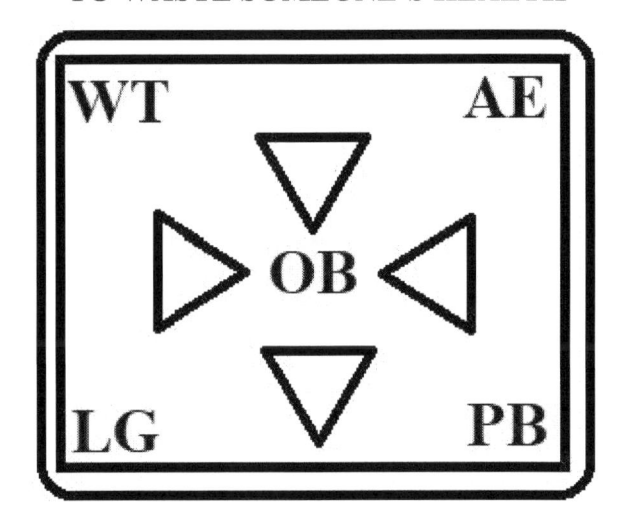

```
WT                    AE
         ▽
    ▷   OB   ◁
         ▽
LG                    PB
```

Mark the above seal on lead during the day and hour of Saturn, when the moon is in it's dark half. On the back of the seal, write the name and birthdate of the victim and pray the psalm nine times over it. Bury it in a dung heap.

TO BRING SHAME ON A PERSON

AD BA TEM N.N.
AD BA TEM N.N.
AD BA TEM N.N.

Write the seal on clean parchment, replacing N.N. with the name of the person. Reside the psalm, and then read the words on the seal, followed by the target's name. Repeat this seven times. Leave the seal where the person will come in contact with it.

PSALM 84

TO MAKE A PERSON PINE FOR YOU

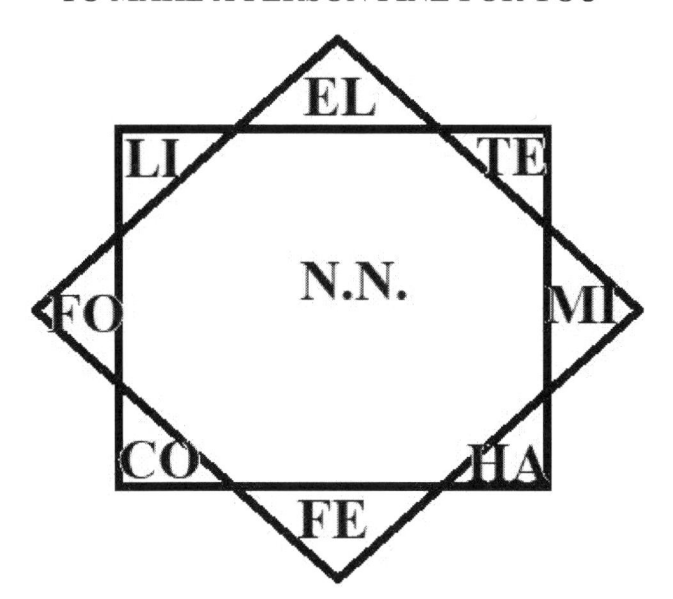

Mark the above seal on copper during the day and hour of Venus, and replace N.N. with the name of the person you seek to enchant, and anoint it with your own blood. Pray the psalm seven times over it, and fumigate it with burning myrtle. Wear it near your heart.

FOR HEART PROBLEMS

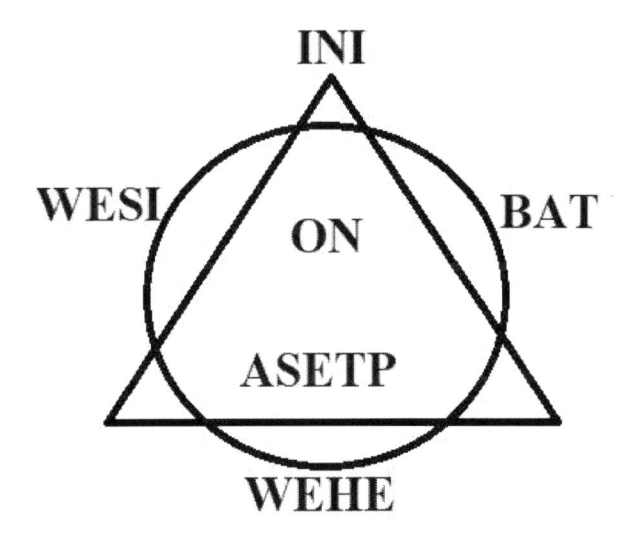

```
        INI
    WESI  ON  BAT
        ASETP
        WEHE
```

Draw the above seal over the chest of the person with charcoal fashioned from oak. Pray the psalm three times over the person, and anoint their forehead, hands, and feet with olive oil in the shape of a cross.

FOR PROTECTION

Carry the above seal on silver, having consecrated it with pure olive oil and the psalm three times, in honor of the Most Holy Trinity.

FOR FAVOR IN COURT

```
┌─────────────────────────┐
│          /\             │
│         /  \            │
│        / EL \           │
│       /      \          │
│      /        \         │
│     / ION DINICTAT \    │
│      \        /         │
│       \      /          │
│        \ BE /           │
│         \  /            │
│          \/             │
└─────────────────────────┘
```

Carry the above seal around your neck, consecrated with the psalm three times and fumigated with myrrh and frankincense.

PSALM 85

TO RESTORE LOST FORTUNE

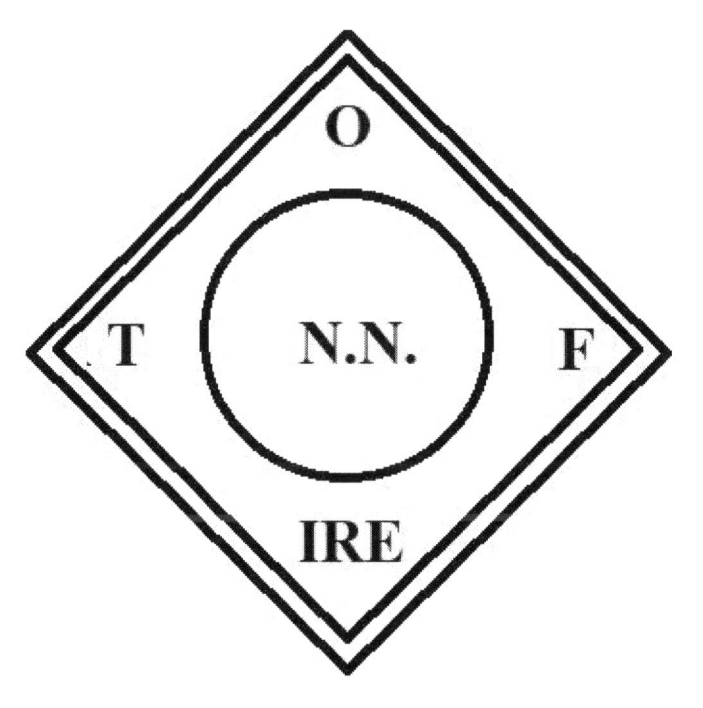

Mark the above seal on a silver or brass plate, replacing N.N. with your name. Whenever the moon is full, catch the light of the moon on the plate and pray the psalm three times. When finished, place it under your mattress or bed.

FOR PEACE IN THE HOME

```
    H P T
    P P P
    T P H
```

Mark the above seal over your door and pray the psalm three times over it in honor of the Most Holy Trinity.

FOR MARITAL FIDELITY

```
   ┌─────────────┐
   │  L.A.F.M.T. │
   │ N.N. et N.N.│
   │  R.A.P.K.E. │
   └─────────────┘
```

Keep the above seal, replacing N.N. and N.N. with your name and your spouse's name, under your mattress, after having consecrated it with the psalm seven times and anointing it with rose oil.

PSALM 86

TO REMOVE POVERTY

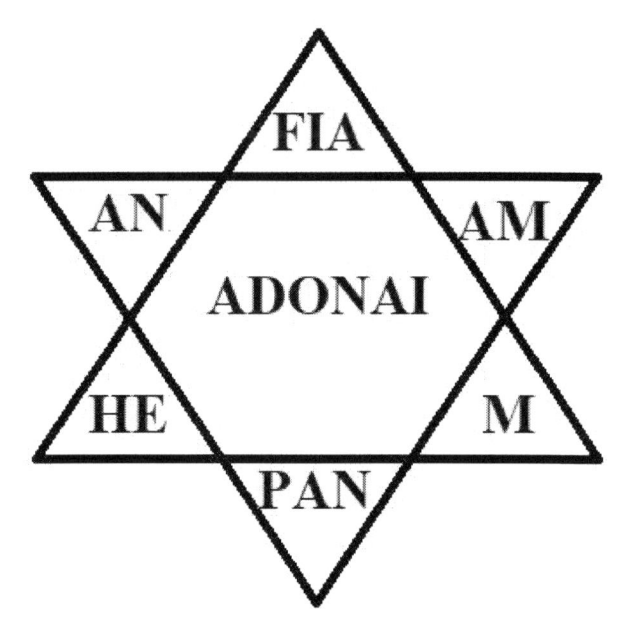

Carry the above seal, on tin, and consecrated with the psalm 8 times. Wear it in your right pocket.

FOR STUDIES

```
┌─────────────────────────┐
│       MIWAT             │
│   ┌─────────────┐       │
│   │   ADONAI    │       │
│   └─────────────┘       │
│       TEM IVV           │
└─────────────────────────┘
```

Mark the above seal on clean parchment on a Sunday and pray the psalm three times over it. Burn it to ashes, and rub the ashes into your scalp.

TO MAKE A PERSON KIND TOWARDS YOU

```
    ╭─────────────────────╮
   │   IAO ON ADONAI      │
   │  ┌───────────────┐   │
   │  │  GIMAS OIGO   │   │
   │  └───────────────┘   │
    ╰─────────────────────╯
```

Mark the above seal in red ink, and on the back write the person's name and birthdate. Pray the psalm devoutly over the seal seven times, and carry it near your heart when you go out around them.

PSALM 87

TO BEGET CHILDREN

```
              BIH
       TOW         ATE
  TOA                    WEH
```

Mark the psalm on copper and anoint it with olive oil. When you go to copulate, touch the seal to your member and pray the psalm seven times.

PSALM 88

TO GAIN A PERSON'S HELP

```
        ETOMICI
         BITI
  N.N. M M P C B Y T Y E T M C  N.N.
         PAIC
         MAM
```

Mark the above seal on clean parchment in blue ink, replacing N.N. and N.N. with your name, and the name of the person whom you seek help from. Pray the psalm six times over the seal, whispering the person's name between each recitation. Keep the seal in your Bible.

TO DESTROY A PERSON

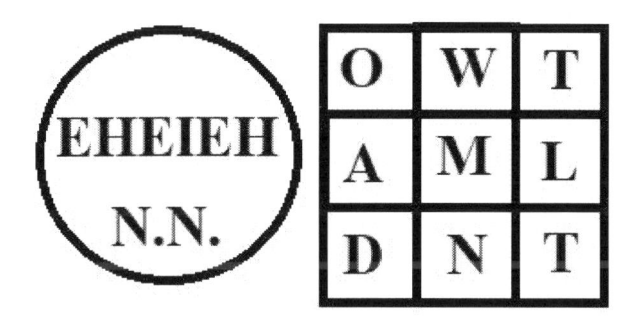

O	W	T
A	M	L
D	N	T

(EHEIEH N.N.)

Mark the above seal on lead with an iron nail on Saturday, during the hour of Mars, the moon increasing. Replace N.N. with the person's name. Recite the psalm nine times over the seal, and hide it where the person will regularly come in contact with it, such as under his porch, bed, desk, etc.

TO TAKE A PERSON'S STRENGTH

```
        EHEIEH
    GWI       TH
      LIKON EWS
       MALEK
         N.N.
         SUR
          ON
```

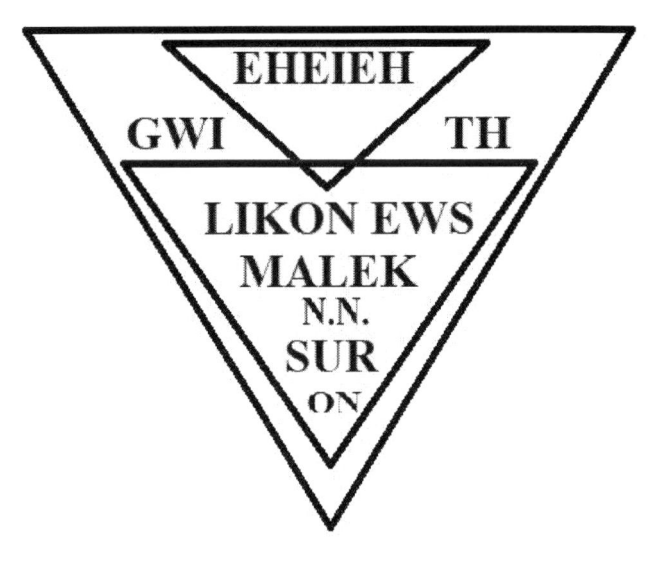

Mark the above seal on parchment, replacing N.N. with the name of the person. Pray the psalm over the seal five times, and place it in a chicken's nest.

TO COMMUNICATE WITH THE DEAD

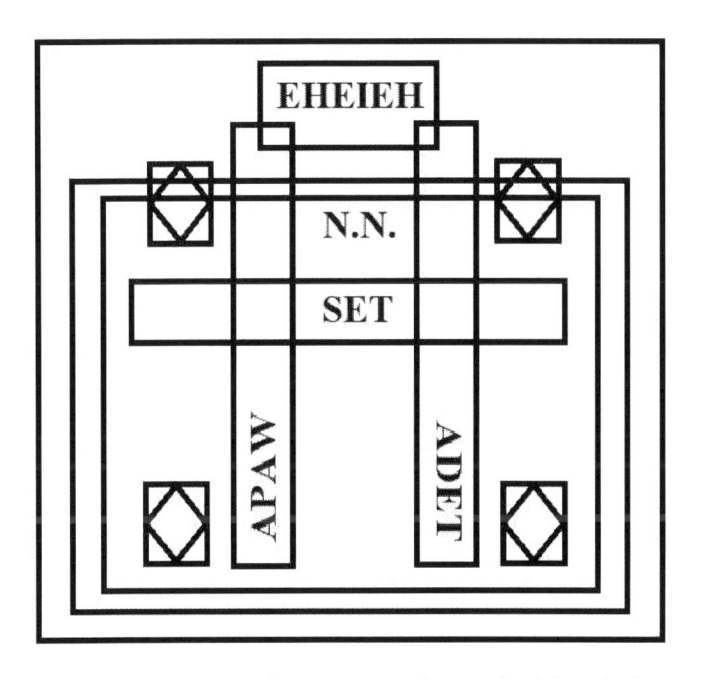

Write the above seal on a new piece of white cloth in red ink, replacing N.N. with the name of the deceased person. Take the cloth to the grave of the deceased and lay it out on the grave. Pray the psalm nine times, stating the name of the deceased nine times after each recitation. Take a pinch of dirt from the grave, and fold it up in the seal. Place the seal under your pillow when you go to sleep.

TO MAKE A PERSON LOSE EVERYTHING

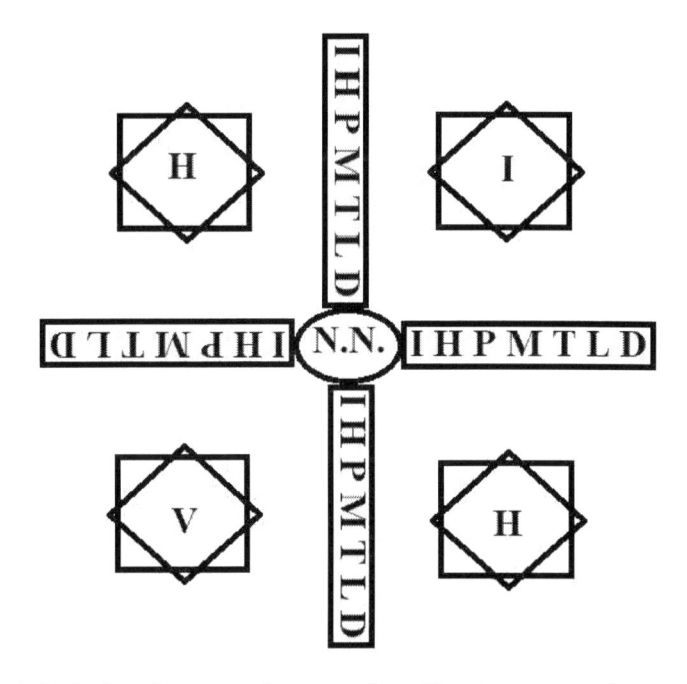

Mark the above seal on a strip of leather, replacing N.N. with the person's name. Pray the psalm nine times over the seal, and place it in a bottle of soured wine. Bury this bottle upside down in an abandoned grave.

TO BREAK FRIENDSHIPS

```
        IAO
   ME   EL   TA
          IHA
   CE    N.N.    IM
          YAH
     OM        ON
          IE
```

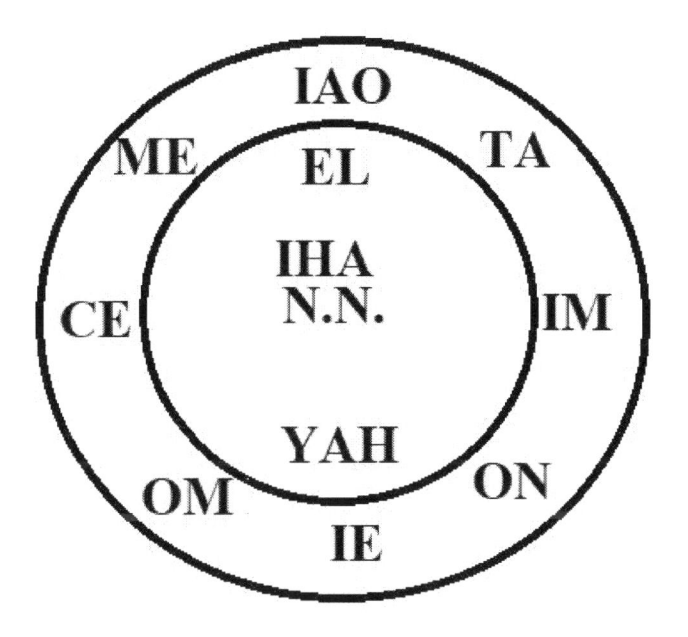

Write the above seal in black ink on a white plate. Pray the psalm five times over it. Build a fire of branches collected from a cemetery and allow it to burn until the plate breaks. When this has happened, take the shards and throw them into a river.

TO PREVENT MOVEMENT

```
        CACE
        N.N.
EHE    DEDO    IEH
        MAT
       ATAM
```

Mark the above seal on parchment, replacing N.N. with the person's name, and wrap it around a piece of the person's hair. Pray the psalm over it nine times, and place it within an iron pot.

TO DAMAGE EYESIGHT

```
        ◇
       YAH
      N.N.
   MIJARE IEDITH
```

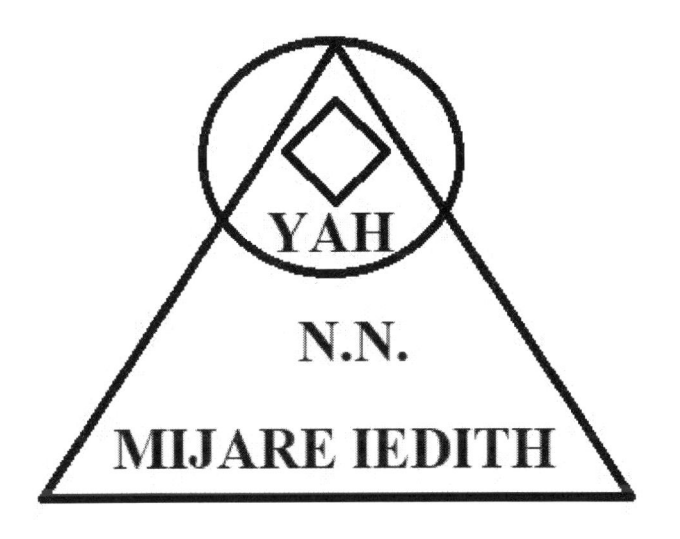

Mark the above seal on a piece of parchment, replacing N.N. with the name of the person. Pray the psalm six times over it, and place it in a mole hill.

TO SUMMON THE SPIRITS OF THE DEAD

```
┌─────────────────────────────┐
│         ANIMUS              │
│  ┌──────────────────────┐   │
│  │ RUA          PI      │   │
│ A│      ◇               │ E │
│ D│    ╱   ╲             │ H │
│ O│  ╱  DIS  ╲           │ E │
│ N│    ╲   ╱             │ I │
│ A│      ◇               │ E │
│ I│ IWT         DTD      │ H │
│  └──────────────────────┘   │
│          YAH                │
└─────────────────────────────┘
```

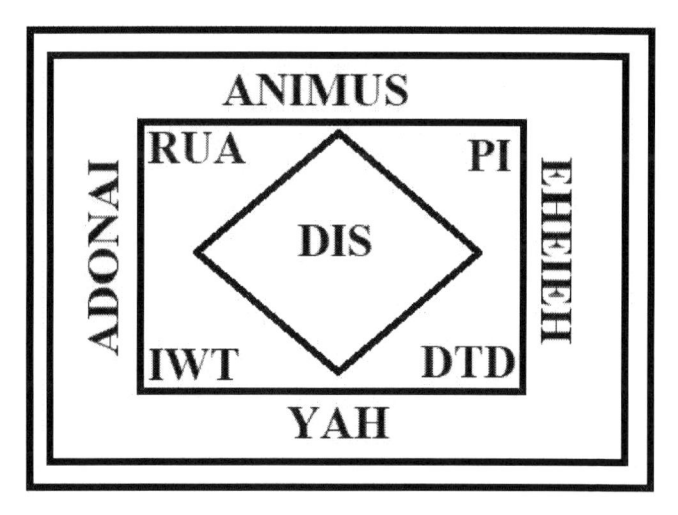

Mark the above seal on lead, and stain it with ochre. Pray the psalm nine times over it and burn a small oil lamp on it in a darkened room.

TO CAUSE NIGHT TERRORS

```
┌─────────────────────────────┐
│   ┌─────────────────────┐   │
│   │    HABI TA DIA      │   │
│   └─────────────────────┘   │
│     IAO ON YAH ABBA         │
└─────────────────────────────┘
```

Consecrate the seal by reciting the psalm three times and fumigating it with sulfur. Hide it in the pillow of the person.

PSALM 89

TO MAKE A PERSON SING YOUR PRAISES

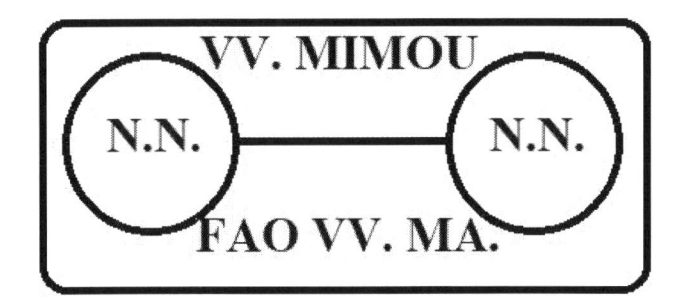

```
VV. MIMOU
N.N. ——————— N.N.
FAO VV. MA.
```

Mark the above seal on clean parchment, replacing the N.N. on the left with your target's name, and the N.N. on the right with your name. Pray the psalm over it every day for seven days straight, and carry the seal next to your skin.

FOR PHYSICAL STRENGTH AND ENDURANCE

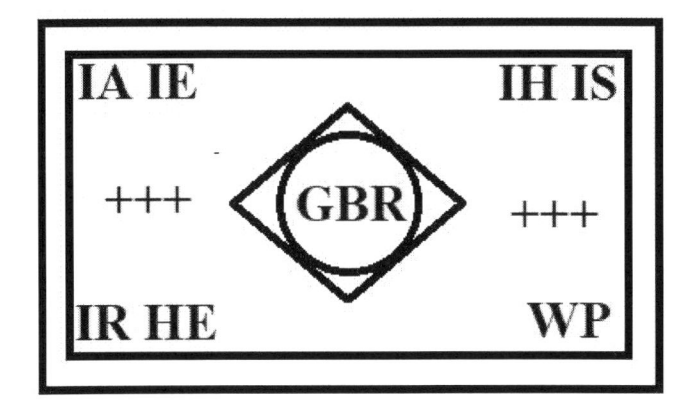

```
IA IE                IH IS
+++    <(GBR)>    +++
IR HE                WP
```

Mark the above seal on a strip of goat's leather, and pray the psalm over it five times. Bind it to your left leg.

FOR VISIONS

```
VAISIOISIAV
    I
    S
    I
    A
    V
```

Wear the above seal, in silver, fumigated with camphor, and consecrated with the psalm three times.

FOR PROMOTIONS AND HONORS

```
┌─────────┐
│ B M F   │
│ A H T   │
│ A I W   │
└─────────┘
```

Carry this seal on brass when seeking promotions, employment, successful applications, etc.
Consecrate it with the psalm eight times, and anoint it with frankincense.

TO CATCH A FUGITIVE

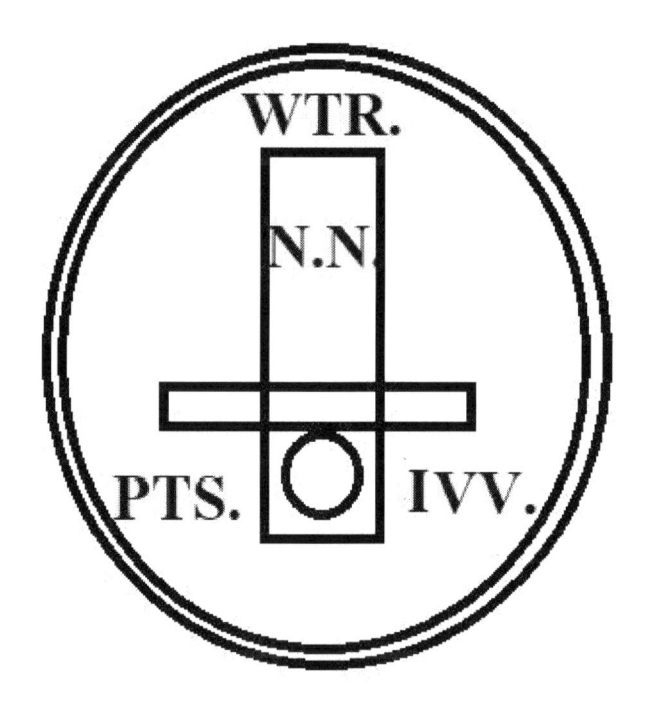

Mark the above seal on a piece of horn or antler, replacing N.N. with the person's name. Pray the psalm over it nine times, fumigating it with sulfur. Bury it under the roots of a tree.

PSALM 90

                    TO KILL

```
I T P B T D S R T D I M
I T P B T D S R T D I
I T P B T D S R T D
I T P B T D S R T
I T P B T D S R
I T P B T D S
I T P B T D
I T P B T
I T P B
I T P
I T
I
```

Mark the above seal on clean parchment in black ink. Every Saturday for nine Saturdays in a row, pray the psalm nine times over the seal. After this has been completed, burn the seal to ashes and sprinkle the ash in his food or drink.

TO KILL SOMEONE IN THEIR SLEEP

IAH ADONAI SADAY ELOHA

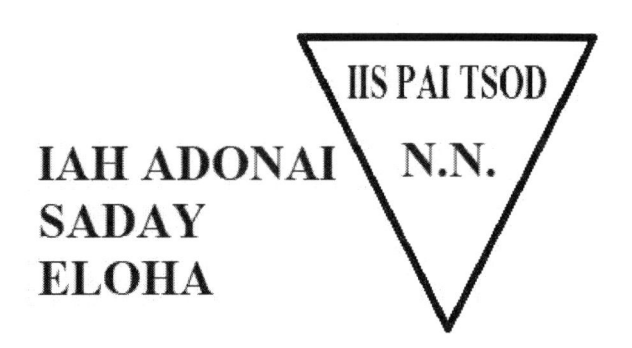

IIS PAI TSOD
N.N.

Mark the above triangle on a piece of goatskin with the Divine Names written on the back, Replace N.N. with the person's name. Every night for nine midnights, pray the psalm nine times over it, speaking the person's name nine times after each recitation. Hide the seal under their bed or in their pillow.

TO KEEP A PERSON DOWN AND OUT

```
┌─────────────────────┐
│      ITM ISV        │
│       NBB           │
│      EII DAW        │
└─────────────────────┘
```
(seal: Star of David with text ITM ISV / NBB / EII DAW inside)

Make the above seal in black ink during the hour of Saturn on Saturday, with the moon decreasing. Pray the psalm nine times over it, reduce it to ashes, and scatter the ashes where they walk.

TO EXPOSE SOMEONE'S SECRET SINS

Mark the above seal on clean parchment in red ink on a Wednesday during the waxing moon. Replace N.N. with the name of the target and recipe the psalm three times over the seal. Hide it near the person's dwelling or work place.

TO DRIVE A PERSON AWAY

```
┌─────────────────────────┐
│  ┌───────────────────┐  │
│  │   FTQ PAW FA      │  │
│  └───────────────────┘  │
│ ┌─────────────────────┐ │
│ │                     │ │
│ │    WEVA PANAS       │ │
│ │   QUI EIR NAE YA    │ │
│ │                     │ │
│ └─────────────────────┘ │
│      ┌─────────┐        │
│      │  N.N.   │        │
│      └─────────┘        │
└─────────────────────────┘
```

Mark the above seal on seven pieces of parchment, replacing N.N. with the name of the person. Take these seals to an abandoned crossroads, and recite the psalm, stating the person's name after. Then cast one of the seals to the ground. Repeat with each seal, then leave without going back.

PSALM 91

FOR PROTECTION

[Seal image: EL ELION / WRI TSO / SHADDAI / WDI TSO]

Carry the above seal, consecrated with the psalm three times, and anointed with pure olive oil.

TO SEE THE PUNISHMENT OF THE WICKED

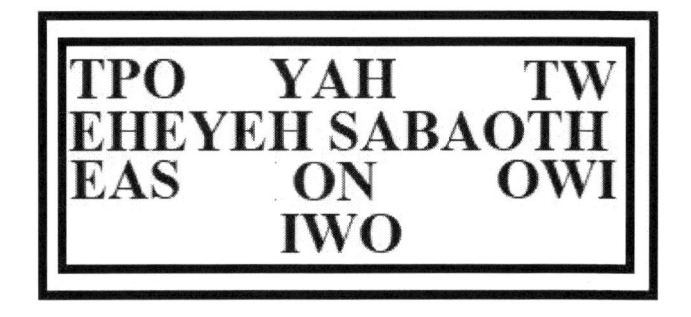

[Seal image:
TPO   YAH   TW
EHEYEH SABAOTH
EAS   ON   OWI
    IWO]

Mark the above seal on parchment and write the name and birthdate of the individual onto it. Set three pinches of sulfur on the seal, and pray the psalm night times and light it. Throw the remaining ashes over the cemetery gate.

AGAINST ANIMAL ATTACKS

```
IWT OTL ATC
IWT TGL ATS
```

Carry the above seal, written in iron gall ink, on clean parchment and fumigated with peppermint. Recite the psalm five times over it.

TO MAKE A PERSON CONTACT YOU

```
       HELAL
        /\
       /  \
      / ON \
     /      \
    /        \
   /   N.N.   \
  /_____\
   MEA IL ANHIM
```

Write the seal on clean parchment, replacing N.N. with the name of the target. Recite the psalm three times, in between stating the person's name, and reading the words on the psalm. Afterwards, burn the seal to ashes, and wave the smoke into your face.

PSALM 92

TO KEEP YOUR PARTNER'S EYE FROM WANDERING

```
┌─────────────────────────────────────┐
│ TEMO         △          AN          │
│           ANI                       │
│      ◁ LEN  □  AIF ▷                │
│           AIUF                      │
│ PROIOU       ▽          PILITM      │
└─────────────────────────────────────┘
```

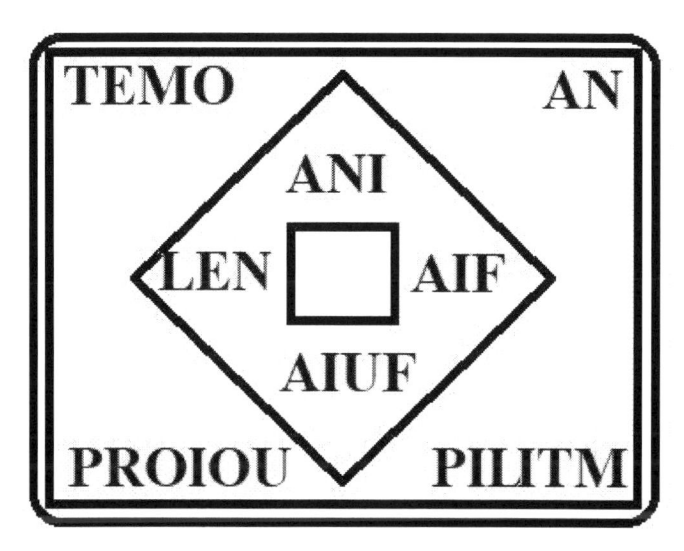

Mark the above seal on a clean piece of cloth, and fold some of your hair and your partner's hair up in it. Recite the psalm seven times over it, and fumigate the package with rose. Place it within an earthenware jar filled with honey and myrtle.

TO MAKE A PERSON IGNORANT AND CONFUSED

```
        ┌─────────────────┐
        │    SEO          │
   NKF  │    SPD          │  DNV
        ├─────────────────┤
  OLDOT │                 │  RESA
        │                 │
        └─────────────────┘
            DOK
```

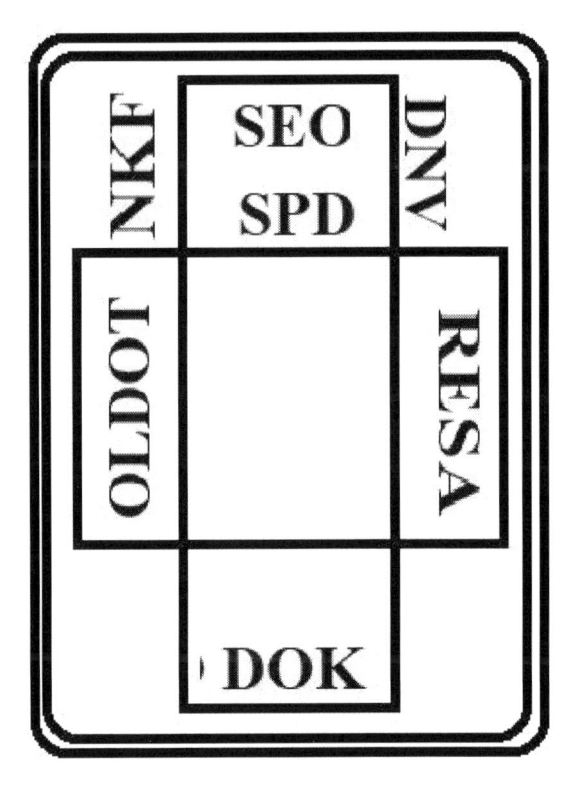

Mark the above seal on clean parchment, writing the person's name and birthdate in the central square. Take nine goose feathers, and tie the seal around it with black thread. Pray the psalm five times over it, and cast it into running water.

FOR PROSPERITY

```
        ACOL
    ┌─────────┐
    │         │
EL  │   WGL   │  GIBOR
┌───┼─────────┼───┐
│ABBA  TRW  PTT YAH│
└───┼─────────┼───┘
    │   FLA   │
    │         │
    └─────────┘
       ELOHIM
```

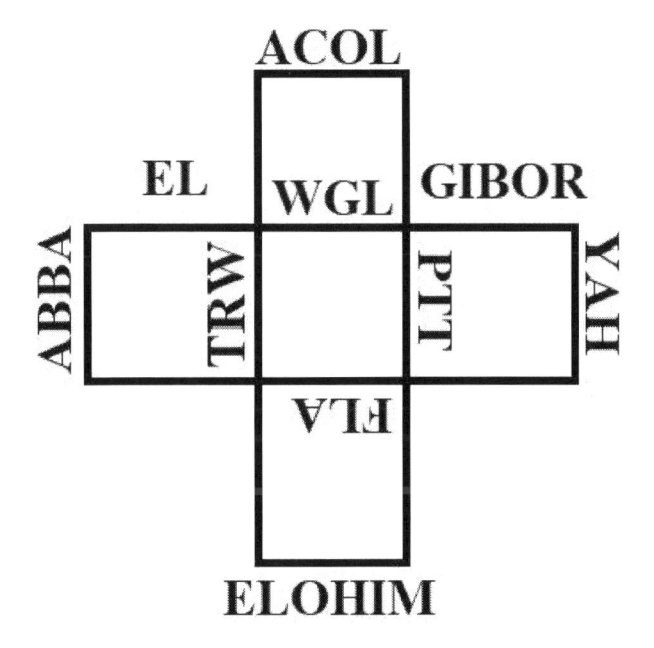

Mark the above seal on clean parchment with ink made from the ashes of palm and holy water. Fumigate the seal with cedar and pray the psalm eight times. Place the seal over your door.

TO MAKE A TREE BEAR FRUIT

```
            AG
      EN
 BFI  STESHA    TWS
      ┌─────┐
  ILA │     │ TEI
      └─────┘
       STAT
       TEI
   WSF        OAT
```

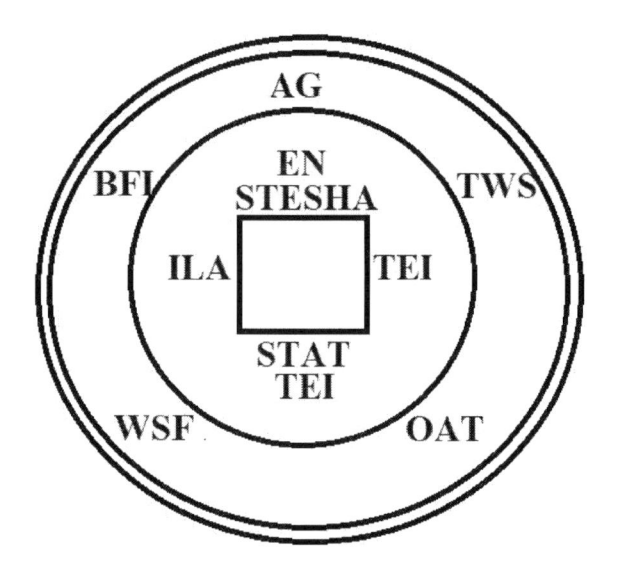

Mark the seal on clean parchment, and pray the psalm three times over it. Bury it under the roots of the tree.

PSALM 93

FOR DOMINATION AND CONTROL

```
      /\
     /UR\
    /GOUA\
   /OMALET\
  / ASTI ON \
 /ITW ELA IAF AE\
```

Carry the above seal, written in red ink, and fumigated with cassia and myrrh. Pray the psalm seven times over it.

PSALM 94

TO CATCH A CRIMINAL

```
     . AIA        IOTE
  VE TERU       PBTT RV



      ATEY    PWTD
      ISV DEO HEA
```

Mark the above seal on lead with an iron nail, on a Saturday in the hour of Mercury. Pray the psalm nine times over it, then bury it at the crime scene. The criminal will be caught.

TO MAKE A PERSON TAKE NOTICE OF A SITUATION

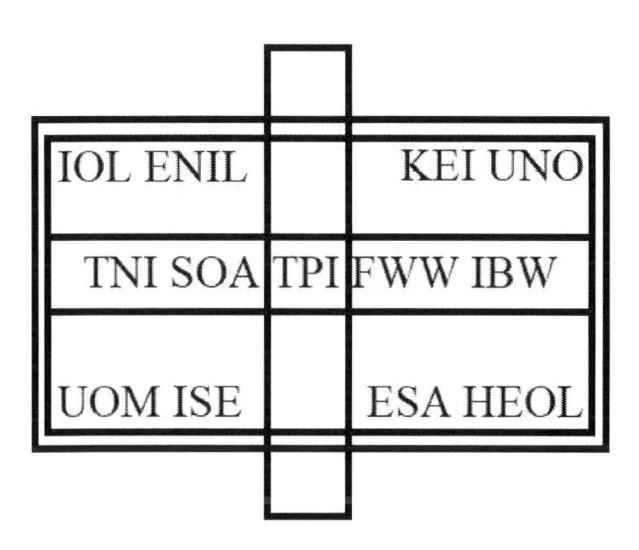

```
┌─────────┬───┬──────────┐
│ IOL ENIL │   │  KEI UNO │
├─────────┼───┼──────────┤
│ TNI SOA │TPI│ FWW IBW  │
├─────────┼───┼──────────┤
│ UOM ISE │   │ ESA HEOL │
└─────────┴───┴──────────┘
```

Mark the above seal in purple ink on clean parchment. Within the top empty square, write the name of the individual. Should you be using the seal to make them notice a person specifically, write their name in the bottom square. Pray the psalm three times over the seal, reading the names written upon it, with your intention held firmly in mind.

TO OVERTURN FALSE JUDGMENTS

```
        /\
   CAC TBA /SEC\ WIA TTB
  ┌──────/────\──────┐
  │ NARU/ ONEA IO\ ARET │
  └────/──────────\────┘
     /SEBOMB IDINO\
```

Mark the above seal on clean parchment in black ink. Under ONEA IO write the name of the judge or arbitrator in the situation. Pray the psalm over it three times every day, while facing the north.

PSALM 95

FOR LUCK IN GAMES

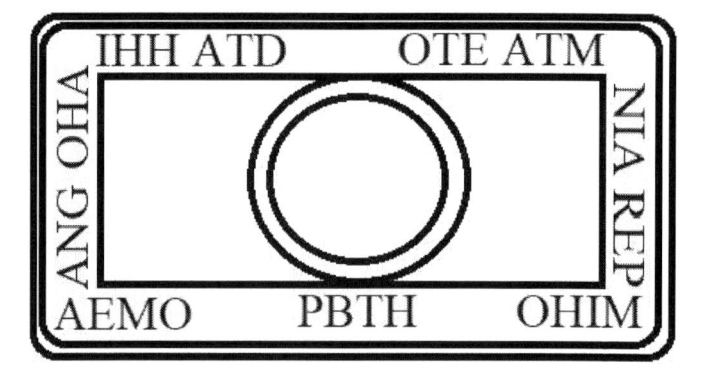

```
    IHH ATD      OTE ATM
  ┌─────────────────────┐
A │         ___         │ N
N │        /   \        │ I
G │       (  O  )       │ A
  │        \___/        │
O │                     │ R
H │                     │ E
A │                     │ P
  └─────────────────────┘
    AEMO    PBTH    OHIM
```

Mark the above seal on clean parchment, writing your name and birthdate within the circle. Fumigate it with camphor and pray the psalm over it seven times. Wear it bound to your left ring finger.

TO ACQUIRE A PERSON'S FORGIVENESS

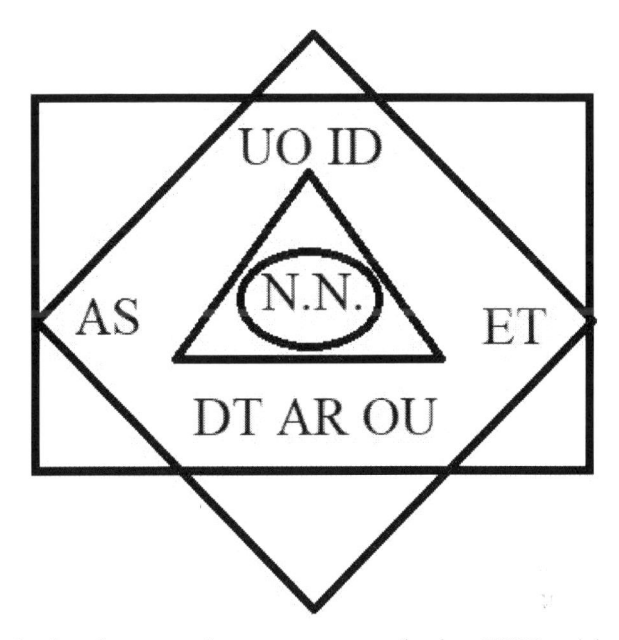

```
         UO ID
    AS   (N.N.)   ET
         DT AR OU
```

Mark the above seal on copper, replacing N.N. with the name of the individual who is angry with you. Fumigate the seal with frankincense and spikenard, and pray the psalm over it three times. Before going to speak to the person, place the seal on your head and read the psalm with your intention held firmly in mind.

PSALM 96

FOR SUCCESS

```
       AO
      IAO
     SAMA
      N.N.
   EA SANCTUS IHS
```

Mark the above seal during a Solar Eclipse on gold, replacing N.N. with your name. Recite the psalm six times over it and fumigate it with frankincense.

TO MAINTAIN YOUR POSITION

```
┌─────────────────────┐
│ IFE    EO     ICA   │
│                     │
│ B              N    │
│ E              E    │
│ M              M    │
│                     │
│ AIT           SIL   │
└─────────────────────┘
```

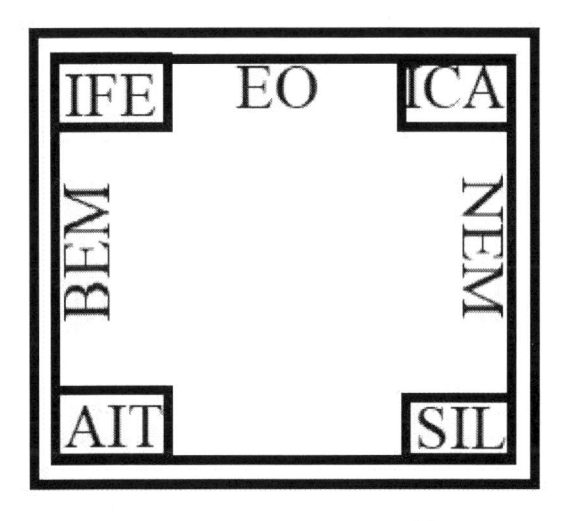

Mark the above seal on green silk with red ink. Should you be invoking the seal for your job, take some soil from the property; to maintain ownership of a home, soil from that property. Fold the soil up into a packet, and pray the psalm five times over it. Bury the seal in a pot of soil and plant a fern over it. Pray the psalm over the plant every day.

PSALM 97

TO PASS UNSEEN

```
         IMEUS
   ◇UNI◇    ◇OHT◇
  ATF   ACA    RAI
           
          N.N.
       
      SEN      ENO
  DSH─────────────CAT
          ◇AUO◇
```

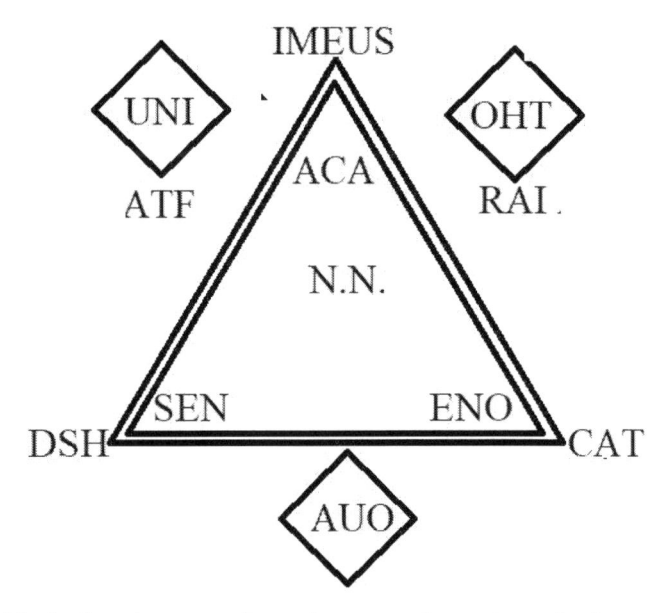

Mark the above seal on clean parchment, replacing N.N. with your name and birthdate. Pray the psalm twenty-eight times over it, and carry it in a vial of mercury. (Mercury is hazardous)

TO DRIVE OUT YOUR ENEMIES BEFORE YOU

```
        ES
       FGB
 AOH [FEOHIM] VID
       ESO
 HAC              HFO
```

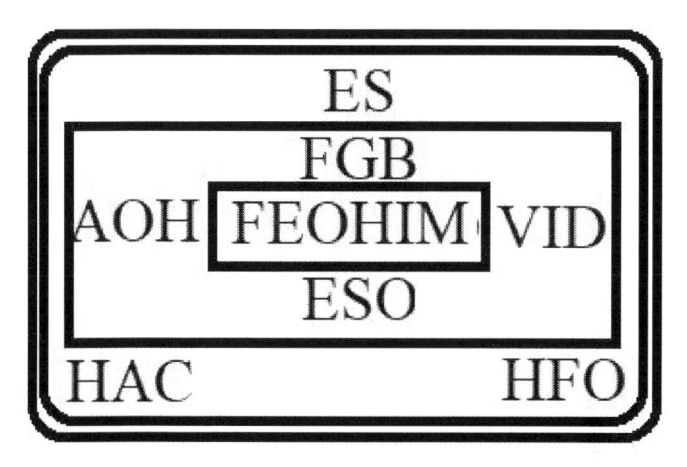

Carry the above seal written in iron gall ink on the day and hour of Mars, and sew it up in red silk. Wear it around the throat, after consecrating it with the psalm five times.

FOR FAME

```
┌─────────────────────────────┐
│  \          HIN GVT ORT  /  │
│   \           HLL       /   │
│    \        ◯◯◯        /    │
│    /        ◯◯◯        \    │
│   /          AES NEMES   \  │
│  /           VTW TES AT   \ │
└─────────────────────────────┘
```

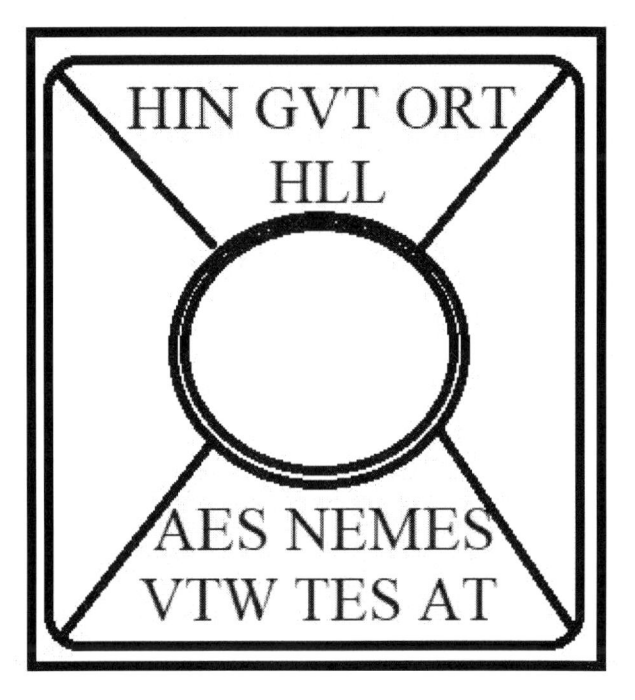

Mark the above seal on clean parchment in gold ink. Within the center of the circle, mark your own initials with your own blood. Pray the psalm six times over it, for six Sundays, fumigating it with frankincense. Carry it near your heart.

TO REMOVE OBSTACLES

Make the above seal in ink fashioned from palm ash and holy water. Replace N.N. with your name. Pray the psalm three times over it and burn it to ashes. Rub the ashes on your feet.

TO MAKE A PERSON DO RIGHT

Mark the above seal on clean parchment with blue ink. Pray the psalm over it seven times, and burn it to ashes in the flame of an oil lamp. Sprinkle the ashes on the person or in their food.

PSALM 98

TO MAKE A PERSON THINK OF YOU

```
┌─────────────────────────────┐
│ HH        BIS         HL    │
│    ┌───────────────────┐    │
│    │   HARE BEH VE     │    │
│    └───────────────────┘    │
│ ES  N.N.    R   N.N.    OV  │
└─────────────────────────────┘
```

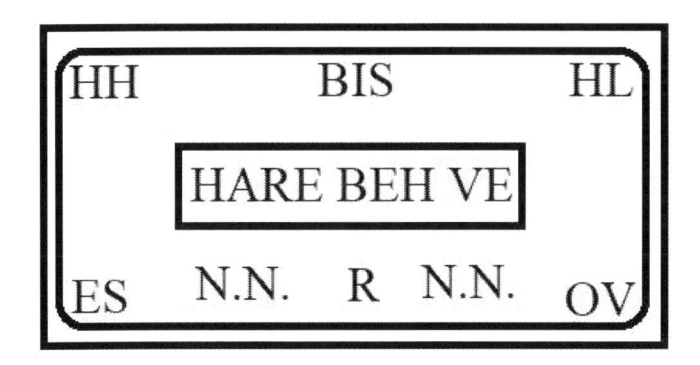

Mark the above seal on a magnolia leaf in gold ink. Replace N.N. and N.N. with your name and the person's name. Pray the psalm three times over it, burn it to ashes, and rub the ashes over your heart.

PSALM 99

TO MAKE PEOPLE ADORE YOU

```
         ┌────┐
         │ AN │
         ├────┤
        ╱│    │╲
       ╱ │    │ ╲
┌─────╱──┼────┼──╲─────┐
│ LTP ╱  │EMAI│   ╲ UEA│
└───╱────┼────┼────╲───┘
   ╱     │    │     ╲
  ╱NOE   │    │   IGA╲
 ╱───────┼────┼───────╲
         │ AM │
         └────┘
```

Mark the above seal on clean parchment in ink of pomegranate juice. Pray the psalm seven times over it, fumigating it with musk. Burn the seal to ashes, and mix it into food or drink that people will eat.

FOR DREAMS

```
┌─────────────────────────────────────┐
│ TFT          POC         HST        │
│                                     │
│         TEM                         │
│              UD                     │
│                                     │
│ ILO          ES          OHE        │
└─────────────────────────────────────┘
```

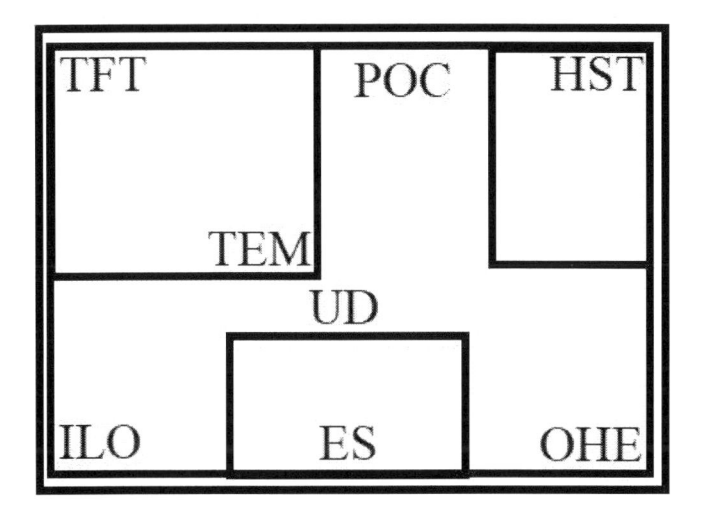

Mark the above seal on clean parchment in purple ink. Fumigate it with camphor and pray the psalm three times over it. Place it under your pillow.

PSALM 100

FOR SUCCESSFUL OPPORTUNITIES

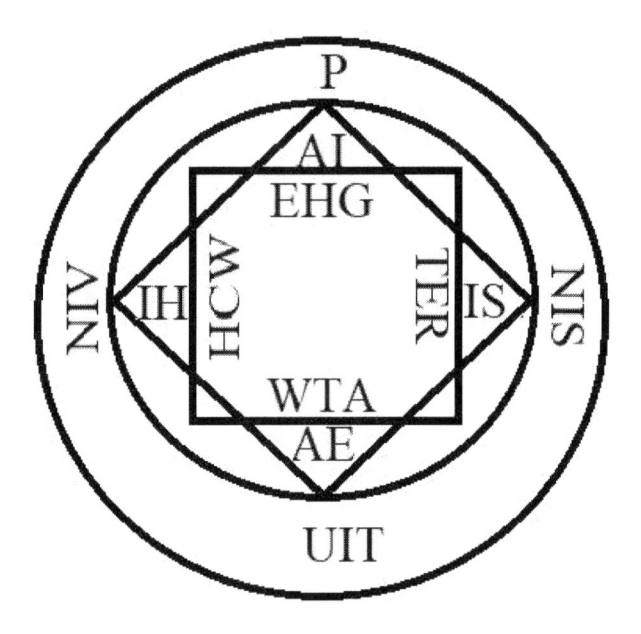

Mark the above seal on clean parchment in green ink. Consecrate it with the psalm seven times and anoint it with pure olive oil. Carry it in your right pocket.

FURTHER READING

Black and White Magic of Doctor Corbeaux Volume 1

A collection of spells, recipes, and workings based on the original classic "Black and White Magic of Marie Laveau." Includes the significance of cards in divination, the use of candles, psalms, roots, and oils

Black and White Magic of Dr. Corbeaux Volume 2

A collection of workings, spells, and recipes for various situations; modeled after the classic "Black and White Magic of Marie Laveau." Included in this volume are rituals with new saints, as well as a form of spider divination.

The Working Girl's Conjure Book: Hoodoo for Hookers

Everyone needs a little conjure in their lives and who more than the industrious working girl? Need protection while out on the job? Want a little something to strum up new business? Need a way to keep the police away? Want to tie down that really rich client? I've got a ritual for that…

SATOR AREPO TENET OPERA ROTAS: Prayers, Rituals, and Charms of Protection, Exorcism, and Uncrossing.

The following text presents a series of rituals, prayers, and charms for the purpose of protection, both physical and spiritual. The reversing of hexes, cleansing, and exorcism prayers will also be discussed.

Handy Human Finger Bones: Haintological Studies Volume 1

Handy Human Finger Bones: Haintological Studies is the first in a series of books where I will discuss subjects involving ghosts, graveyards, and the various beliefs and conjures relating to them. Over the course of these volumes, we will be discussing everything from power hotspots in cemeteries, how to conjure or expel the spirits of the dead, the materia magica of the graveyard, the occult significance of various human bones, and other folklore relating to the spirits of the dead in general.

Cartomancy 2.0: Further Studies in Cartomancy

In 2011 I wrote "Cartomancy; Divination with Playing Cards" (http://www.lulu.com/shop/dr-lazarus-corbeaux/cartomancy-divination-with-playing-cards/paperback/product-17990527.html) as an introductory bare bones extremely basic text on beginning divination with 54 playing cards. I was never really happy with my early books, and I have wanted to publish an update to my cartomancy book, with extended card meanings and spreads. To avoid repetitiveness, I will skip over the preliminary information that I have previously discussed in "Cartomancy; Divination with Playing Cards" and move directly on to the material I wish I had added in the original, as well as other helpful hints I never included in the original book. For those of you who have already read my previous book, you will be aware of the card correspondence regarding various saints and biblical events. In this text, I will include more correspondences, and include information on how the individual practitioner can graft the various spirits or deities they work with into the cards themselves.

Love Conjures: A Collection of Spiritual Works for Love and Relationships

What follows is a collection of recipes, workings, and advice to assist in the working of conjure for love, attraction, fidelity, and control for the use of individuals, both male and female, and of whatever sexual orientation.Before you make use of any of the herbs or materials referenced in this work, make sure you are not allergic. The key to success in conjuring a partner is to never get caught. Tell no one what you're doing, never let anyone see you doing it, and never admit to it. Often, though not always, should your target become aware of what you are doing, your works will falter - whether for psychological suggestion in the mind of the conjured, or through some esoteric principle inherent in love working, no one could say definitively. All I can say, it has been my experience that it is best to never let your target know that they are being, or have been conjured.

Santisima Muerte Trilogy: Altars, Prayers, and Rituals...with added materials

A trilogy of my original three books on the subject of the Santisima Muerte with added materials. Subjects included: how to erect an altar and work with the Santisima Muerte; recipes, rituals, and divination techniques to assist in communication with the saint.

Narco-Conjure Volume 1: Spells, Charms, and Formulas for Drug Dealers

What follows is a collection of prayers, charms, spells, rituals, formulas and folklore that may be of use to the purveyor of fine controlled substances for assistance in their economic endeavors. Need 5.0 off your back? Business too slow? Need some added protection on the street? Got a friend or employee in jail? Need to influence a court case? All this and more will be discussed

Black Magic for Kids: A Beginner's Guide to Hexes

There's no reason hexes, curses, and jinxes have to be complicated. Black Magic for Kids: A Beginner's Guide to Hexes presents a list of rituals, formulas, and prayers that are easily performed by the novice of all ages.

Black Magic for Kids Volume 2

Volume 2 of Black Magic for Kids contains the names, symbols, and rituals for employing the use of various evil spirits for practical purposes. Slightly more complex than Volume 1, but still an easy usable manual for the aspiring practitioner of the black arts.

Pum Pum Conjure: Attracting Women Through Conjure

A collection of charms, spells, and recipes for men to use for the sole purpose of attracting the romantic interests of ladies.

DIVINATION AND SPIRITUAL WORK

Copyright 2019 Dr. Corbeaux

If you would like to contact the author for divination or spiritual work, forward all questions to drcorbeaux@gmail.com

Author Page:
http://www.amazon.com/author/gedelazarus